HYCU College English 1

김남희

- 중앙대학교 영어학 학사
- 중앙대학교 영어영문학 석사 (영어교육 전공)
- 미국 The Pennsylvania State University 영어교육학 박사
- 한양사이버대학교 영어학과 전임교수

문도식

- 서울대학교 영문학 학사 / 석사
- 미국 University of Illinois at Urbana-Champaign 영어교육학 석사 / 박사
- 서울대학교 대학영어 강의교수
- 한양사이버대학교 영어학과 전임교수

박수정

- 계명대학교 학사 (미국학 전공 / 영어영문학 부전공)
- 미국 University of Illinois at Urbana-Champaign 영어교육학 석사 / 박사
- 미국 University of Illinois at Urbana-Champaign TESOL 석사 프로그램 객원강사
- 한양사이버대학교 영어학과 전임교수

HYCU College English 1

지은이 | 김남희 · 문도식 · 박수정

초판 1쇄 발행 | 2013년 8월 29일

초판 3쇄 발행 | 2016년 3월 31일

발행인 | 이영무 발행처 | 한양대학교출판부

주소 | 서울 성동구 왕십리로 222

전화 | 02 2220 1432~4 팩스 | 02 2220 1435

홈페이지 | press.hanyang.ac.kr 전자우편 | presshy@hanyang.ac.kr

출판등록 | 제4-7호(1972년 2월 29일) 인쇄처 | (주)네오프린텍

ISBN 978-89-7218-430-0 93740

HYCU
College English 1

Forward

본 교재 HYCU College English 1 은 국제 공용어로서의 영어의 중요성이 증대하고 있는 시대의 요구에 부응하여 영어 능력을 체계적이고 균형 있게 발전시킬 수 있도록 하기 위해서 기획되었습니다. 본 교재가 제시하고 있는 다양한 활동을 통해서 학습자들은 실용적인 영어 의사소통 기능을 향상시킬 수 있을 뿐만 아니라 다양한 소재와 형식의 읽기 자료를 통해서 교양과 국제적인 감각 및 타 문화에 대한 이해도를 높일 수 있을 것으로 기대합니다.

본 교재는 생활양식, 인물, 언어, 문화의 4가지 큰 주제로 구성이 되어있습니다. 각 주제에 관련된 다양한 읽을 거리를 중심으로 영어의 네 가지 기능인 읽기, 말하기, 듣기와 쓰기를 균형 있게 공부할 수 있도록 구성되어 있습니다. 효과적인 영어 학습을 위해 각 단원은 다음과 같은 순서로 구성되어 있습니다.

- Warm Up: 각 과의 주제와 관련된 질문 및 대화문
- Vocabulary Preview: 새로 나오는 어휘 및 표현 연습
- Let's Read it Together: 생활양식, 인물, 언어, 문화와 관련된 교양적인 내용의 글
- Reading Comprehension: 본문 이해도를 측정하기 위한 내용 이해 문제 및 읽기 전략
- Vocabulary Preview: 문맥을 통한 어휘 확인 문제
- Grammar Focus: 교재의 본문에 나오는 주요 문법 사항에 대한 설명과 연습문제
- Let's Talk About It: 각 단원의 내용과 관련된 대화와 자주 사용되는 어휘와 표현
- Common Errors in English: 한국 학습자들이 자주 범하는 영어 표현의 오류와 설명

또한 책의 뒷 부분에는 본문 읽기 지문의 번역 및 각 활동의 해답과 어휘 목록 그리고 문법 사항들을 첨가해서 학생들이 자율적으로 학습하는데 도움이 되도록 했습니다.

본 교재 출간을 위해 영어 원어민 감수를 해 주신 Reginald Lee 교수님과 편집을 위해 애써 주신 한양대학교 출판부 편집부 직원들께 감사를 드립니다.

2013년 8월

저자들 씀

CONTENTS

Lesson 1
YOU ARE WHAT YOU EAT

CONTENTS

Reading: 건강에 좋은 음식과 식습관에 관한 사항들

Reading Strategy: 요지 찾기

Word Power: 명사 + −al

Grammar Focus: 명령문

Let's Talk About It: 제안/상황에 대한 감탄

Common Errors in English: Cooker vs. Cook

WARM UP

A. 아래 그림을 보고 질문에 답하시오.

1. Which one do you usually like to eat?
2. In your opinion, which food is not good for your health?
3. Do you know how to eat a balanced meal?

B. 대화를 듣고 질문에 답하시오.

Sujin: Karen, I think I gained weight. What should I do?
Karen: What kind of food do you usually eat?
Sujin: I like to eat chocolate, peanut butter, and hamburgers.
Karen: How many meals do you eat a day?
Sujin: I have three meals but I also like to have snacks like cookies and chocolate.
Karen: Sujin, you need to watch your eating habits first.

1. What kind of food does Sujin like to eat?
2. How many meals does Sujin eat a day?
3. What does Sujin need to do to be healthy?

vocabulary

gain weight (체중이 늘다) like (동사: ~를 좋아하다/전치사: ~처럼)
a day (하루에, a = per ~당)

VOCABULARY PREVIEW

A. 단어의 뜻과 표현을 공부해 보세요

1. contain (포함하다)	to have something inside

This food contains essential nutrients. (이 음식은 기초 영양소가 들어 있다.)

2. reduce (줄이다)	to make something smaller

It reduces the risks of heart disease. (그것은 심장병의 위험을 줄여 준다.)

3. illness (질병)	to be sick

Many people died from illness. (많은 사람들이 병으로 죽었다.)

4.prevent (막다, 예방하다)	to stop or to keep from happening

Prevent the spread of the rumor. (소문이 퍼지는 것을 막아라.)

5. maintain (유지하다)	to keep something at the same level

maintain a good relationship (좋은 관계를 유지하다)

6. essential (절대로 필요한)	basic or necessary

essential to maintain the role (그 역할을 유지하는데 필수적인)

7. consume (섭취하다)	to eat or drink

Consume 1,500 calories a day to lose weight. (체중을 줄이기 위해서 하루에 1500칼로리를 섭취하라.)

8. increase (증가하다)	to become more

Do not increase the amount of salt intake. (소금 섭취량을 늘이지 마시오.)

9. chew (씹다)	to bite with the teeth

Don't chew gum in school. (학교에서는 껌을 씹지 마시오.)

10. tip (조언)	a suggestion or hint

These are tips to help you study. (이것들이 당신이 공부하는데 도움이 되는 조언들이다.)

B. 빈칸에 알맞은 표현을 넣으시오.

such as,	Cut down on,	when it comes to,	start off,	take time
(~와 같은)	(줄이다)	(~에 관하여서)	(시작하다)	(여유를 가지다)

1. ( ) the portions of each meal.
2. Carbohydrates are found in food ( ) rice, bread, and potatoes.
3. Eat breakfast because it is the best way to ( ) your day.
4. Here are some things we need to consider ( ) food and eating.
5. During your meal, ( ) to chew your food and stop eating before you feel full.

LET'S READ IT TOGETHER

You are what you eat

1 Have you ever heard of the saying, "You are what you eat"? It means that the food we eat affects our health. Here are some things we need to consider when it comes to our choices of food and eating habits.

2 A healthy and balanced diet helps maintain or improve our health. So our meals should contain essential nutrients such as carbohydrates, fats, proteins, minerals, and vitamins. Carbohydrates are the main source of the body's energy and are found in food such as rice, bread, and potatoes. We also need good fat to keep our body strong and to prevent diseases. Good sources of healthy fat that our body needs include nuts, seeds, olives, and fish such as salmon.

3 Protein builds and maintains muscles and organs of our body. Meat, fish, poultry, and eggs are important sources of protein. Fish can reduce the risk of heart disease. However, red meat and butter contain lots of saturated fat which can increase the risk of diseases. Minerals and vitamins are also essential to our bodies. For example, fruit and vegetables are rich in minerals and vitamins that protect us from some types of illnesses such as cancer and high blood pressure.

salmon

poultry

meat

Quick Comprehension Questions

1. What are essential nutrients?
2. Where can you find healthy fats?
3. What are rich in minerals and vitamins?

vocabulary

consider(고려하다) improve(향상시키다) nutrients(영양소) risk(위험)
carbohydrate(탄수화물) protein(단백질) disease(질병) include(포함하다)

4 Our eating habits are as important as choosing the right, healthy food. Here are some tips for eating smart. First, think about planning a healthy diet that contains essential nutrients. When you go grocery shopping, choose vegetables, fruit, whole grains, and things that contain good sources of protein and healthy fat. Second, limit your sugar and salt intake. Sugar makes your energy go through quick ups and downs. Salt itself is not bad but remember most Koreans consume too much salt in their diet.

grains

5 Third, cut down on the portions of each meal. When you eat out, don't order too much of anything. At home, using smaller plates is a good idea. Fourth, during your meal, take time to chew your food and stop eating before you feel full. It takes a few minutes for your brain to tell your body that you have had enough food. Finally, eat breakfast because it is the best way to start off your day. Remember eating small and healthy meals throughout the day keeps your energy up.

plate

Quick Comprehension Questions

1. Which items are necessary for eating smart?
2. How should you eat your meals?
3. How does sugar work in the body?

vocabulary

smart(똑똑한)	grocery(식료품)	meal(끼니, 식사)
whole grain(통 곡물)	portion(음식의 1인분)	intake(섭취, 섭취량)

READING COMPREHENSION

A. Understanding the Main Idea: 본문의 요지로 알맞은 것을 고르시오.

1. We need to eat less.
2. We have to have good eating habits.
3. Choosing good food and good eating habits will make us healthy.
4. Small portions are a tip to maintain good health.

B. Text Organization

박스 안에는 읽기 지문들의 주제들이 요약되어 있다.아래 문장의 적절한 주제를 고르시오.

a. Essential nutrients: proteins
b. Essential nutrients: carbohydrates
c. Essential nutrients: fats
d. Essential nutrients: vitamins and minerals
e. Choosing healthy food
f. Eating habits

___ 1. When you go grocery shopping, choose vegetables, fruit, whole grains, and things that contain good sources of protein and healthy fats.
___ 2. They are found in food such as rice, bread, and potatoes.
___ 3. For example, vegetables and fruits are rich in these.
___ 4. During your meal, take time to chew your food and stop eating before you feel full.
___ 5. Good sources of these include nuts, seeds, olives, and fish such as salmon.
___ 6. Fish, poultry, and eggs are important sources of these.

C. Understanding Details:
아래의 문장이 본문의 내용과 맞으면 T, 틀리면 F를 선택하시오.

	True	False
1. Fats are found in bread and potatoes.		
2. Fish will increase the risk of disease.		
3. You need to take time to chew your food.		
4. Eating breakfast is the best way to start off your day.		
5. Salt will make your energy go through quick ups and downs.		
6. Shopping is a good way to plan a healthy diet.		

D. Reading Strategy

요지 찾기 (Finding Main Ideas)

요지 (main idea)는 독자에게 전달하고자 하는 핵심 내용이다. 대개는 주제문 (topic sentence)으로 제시되지만 분명하게 드러나지 않아 독자가 추론해야 하는 경우도 있다. 요지파악이 힘든 경우 먼저 주제 (topic)를 파악하고 글쓴이가 주제에 대해 하고자 하는 말이 무엇인지를 생각하는 것이 도움이 된다. 긴 글의 경우 소제목을 활용하여 부분의 요지를 파악하고 이를 종합하여 글 전체의 요지를 파악할 수 있다.

아래 문단의 요지를 고르시오.

A healthy and balanced diet helps maintain or improve our health, and should contain essential nutrients such as carbohydrates, fats, proteins, minerals, and vitamins. Carbohydrates are the main source of the body's energy and are found in food such as rice, bread, and potatoes. We also need good fats to keep our bodies strong and to prevent diseases. Good sources of healthy fat that our bodies needs include nuts, seeds, olives, and fish such as salmon.

__ 1. A healthy and balanced diet contains essential nutrients.
__ 2. Eating habits are important for our health.
__ 3. There are five types of essential nutrients.
__ 4. Good sources of healthy fat are important.

VOCABULARY REVIEW

A. 빈칸에 알맞은 단어를 넣으시오.

essential	consume	chew	contain	reduce	tip	prevent	maintain

1. You need to ____________ sugar intake to be healthy.
2. They ____________ too much sugar and salt in their diets.
3. Healthy food can help ____________ illness.
4. You need to eat well to ____________ your health.
5. Please ____________ your gum quietly.
6. These boxes ____________ many interesting things.
7. A good ____________ to be healthy is to eat well.
8. Carbohydrates, fats, and proteins are ____________ nutrients for our body.

B. Word Power

명사+ –al = 형용사

명사에 –al 접미사를 붙혀서 형용사를 만든다. 명사가 모음으로 끝나는 경우는 (예: face, essence) 접미사의 모음과의 음운현상에 의해서 어휘 끝의 모음이 탈락되거나 변형되는 경우가 발생한다.

essence (본질.기초) + al ⇨ essential (절대필요한)
person (사람) + al ⇨ personal (사람의)
nation (국가) + al ⇨ national (국가의)
music (음악) + al ⇨ musical (음악의)
face (얼굴) + al ⇨ facial (얼굴의)

1. I think that good eating habits are **essential** to being healthy.
2. The boy made a funny **facial** expression.
3. The Bald Eagle is the U.S. **national** bird symbol.
4. A piano is a **musical** instrument.

GRAMMAR FOCUS

Imperatives (명령문)

명령문 명령을 할 때 주로 사용이 되는 문장이다. 명령문은 주어 You 가 생략이 되고 동사의 원형으로 시작한다. 문장 앞에 please를 넣어 사용하기도 한다. 부정을 나타낼 때는 동사 앞에 Don't (또는 Do not)을 넣고, 강조할 때는 Do를 넣는다. 명령문의 사용은 명령, 제안, 지시를 할 때, 용기를 줄 때, (잘되는) 바램을 나타낼 때 등이 있다.

Try again.

Please eat healthy food.

Limit your sugar and salt intake.

명령	지시나 제안
Be quiet Tell me the truth Don't make noise in here.	Enjoy your meal. Think about planning a healthy diet. Have some more coffee.

A. 다음 문장들을 읽고, 각각의 상황에 맞는 명령문 형태의 문장들을 만들어 보시오.

1. When you want to tell your students to be quiet in the classroom.

   ____

2. When you give advice to Minho about not eating saturated fat.

   Minho, ______________________________

B. 다음 글을 읽고 틀린 부분을 찾아 맞게 고치시오.

To keep your body healthy, a healthy diet is very important. First, should be careful when you choose food. Second, learning about essential nutrients before grocery shopping. Third, please limiting your sugar and salt intake. Also, not eat food that contains unhealthy fat. When you have meals, have chew your food and stopped eating before you feel full.

LET'S TALK ABOUT IT

A. 다음 대화를 듣고 연습해 봅시다.

Karen: Joon, do you want to eat out tonight?
Joon: I'd like to but I need to lose weight.
Karen: Why? You don't look overweight
Joon: Well, the doctor said I am.
Karen: You should try eating smaller meals.
Joon: I've tried, but I just can't seem to stop eating snacks between meals.
Karen: Why don't you eat more fruit and vegetables instead?
Joon: **That's a good idea.** I'll try it.

B. 유용한 표현들

1. 제안, 권유나 어떤 상황에 대납하는 표현은 상황에 알맞게 사용해야 한다.

· 제안을 받아들일 때 :
Yes, Ok/ All right 등이 있고 미국영어에서는 **Sure!**를 사용하기도 한다. 그 외에도 **That's a good idea, That sounds great!** (그것 좋은 생각이다), Great! (대단하다), **That's terrific!** (멋지다) 등이 있다. (이 표현들은 어떤 상황에 대한 감탄을 표시할 때도 사용된다.)

· 거절 할때:
No, thank you (고맙지만 됐습니다.), **I'd love to, but..** (그러고 싶지만…), **I don't feel like it** (그럴 기분이 아니에요.) 등을 사용한다.

2. 거절을 할 때는 거절의 이유를 말하거나 다른 것을 제안하는 것이 더 정중하다.

이때 사용하는 표현으로는 How about… instead? (대신 ..하는 것이 어떨까?) 또는 I'd rather (=I would rather)+ 동사원형 (나는 ..하는게 낫겠어) 등이 있다.

How about eating out **instead**? (대신 외식하는 것이 어떨까?)
I'd rather return to Korea. (나는 한국으로 돌아가는 것이 낫겠어.)

C. 말해보기: 아래 빈칸에 알맞은 표현을 넣으시오.

1. A: We are going ice skating. Do you want to come?
(우리 스케이트 타러 갈 건데. 너 갈거니?)
B: ______________________. I'd love to. (좋은 생각이야. 나도 가고 싶어)

2. A: Hey Karen, great news, I found a job and I start tomorrow!
(케런, 좋은 소식이야, 나 직업 구했어 내일 시작할 거야)
B: Wow, John, ______________________. (와, 존, 멋지다!)

Cooker vs. Cook

Sujin: Chris, my mother really cooks well. She is an excellent cooker.
Chris: What? Sujin, a **cooker** is **a thing** used to cook food, so we don't say a person is a cooker.
Sujin: Oh, really? Which word should I use then?
Chris: Cook. You can say, "My mother is an excellent **cook**.'

1. Cook은 '요리하다'는 동사로 쓰이지만 '요리사'라는 명사의 뜻도 있다.

   A person who is a highly skilled **cook** is called a **chef**.
   (실력이 아주 좋은 요리사는 쉐프 라고 불린다.)
   *Chef는 직업이 요리사로 주로 호텔이나 식당의 주방장을 말할 때 사용한다.

   음식 만드는 일이나 특정한 방식으로 만든 요리를 말할 때는 cooking 을 사용한다.

   Baking, frying, boiling, and smoking are different methods of **cooking**.
   (굽기, 튀기기, 끓이기, 훈제는 요리의 다른 방법들이다.)

2. 명사에 접미사 -er을 붙이면 '~하는 사람'의 뜻이 된다 하지만 cook의 경우는 -er를 붙이면 '요리기구'를 의미한다.

   Most Koreans own a rice **cooker**.
   (대부분의 한국사람들은 밥솥을 가지고 있다.)

Lesson 2
LET'S WORK OUT

CONTENTS

Reading: 건강유지를 위한 운동과 방법

Reading Strategy: 훑어 읽기와 찾아 읽기

Word Power: 형용사 + -ity

Grammar Focus: 비교급

Let's Talk About It: 희망과 소원을 표현하기

Common Errors in English: Hiking vs. Mountain Climbing

WARM UP

A. 아래 그림을 보고 질문에 답하시오.

1. Which exercise above will help your body to be more flexible?
2. Which type of exercise do you prefer to do?
3. Which exercise will make your muscles strong?

B. 대화를 듣고 질문에 답하시오.

Chris: Minho, I've decided to lose weight, so I'm going to eat healthy food.
Minho: Good to hear that. But you also need to exercise to be healthy.
Chris: I know. But I'm really busy so I don't have time to do it.
Minho: You can exercise at home. Stretching is a good exercise.
Chris: Oh, that will save time. I'll try it tonight.

1. What is Chris going to do to lose weight?
2. Why doesn't Chris have time to exercise?
3. Which exercise is good to do at home?

vocabulary

Good to hear that. (정말 잘 됐다. It is 가 앞에 생략된 문구)
lose weight (체중을 줄이다) save time (시간을 절약하다)

VOCABULARY PREVIEW

A. 단어의 뜻과 표현을 공부해 보세요.

1. physical (신체의)	of the body as opposed to the mind
Physical activity promotes good health. (신체활동은 건강을 증진 시킨다.)	
2. flexibility (유연성)	ability to bend without breaking
Stretching helps improve your flexibility. (스트레칭은 유연성을 증가하는데 도움이 된다.)	
3. prefer (좋아하다)	to like better or more
I prefer bright colored clothing. (나는 밝은색의 옷을 더 좋아한다.)	
4. deliver (배달하다)	to carry and leave at the proper place
We deliver it to your home. (우리는 그것을 당신의 집으로 배달합니다.)	
5. involve (포함하다)	to have as a part of include
This job involves hard work. (이 일은 힘든 작업을 포함하고 있다.)	
6. injury (상처.부상)	to be physically hurt
an injury to one's shoulder (…의 어께 부상)	
7. strengthen (강화하다)	to make stronger
These exercises will strengthen your back muscles. (이 훈련들은 등 근육을 강화시킬 것 이다.)	
8. workout (신체활동,운동)	physical exercise
We should do a 30 minute aerobic workout. (우리는 30분간의 유산소 운동을 해야 한다.)	
9. burn (태우다)	on fire or to reduce calories
Jogging can help you burn more calories. (조깅은 더 많은 칼로리를 태우는 것을 도울 수 있다.)	
10. instead (대신에)	in the place of someone or of something
You can use milk instead of cream. (당신은 크림 대신 우유를 쓸 수 있다.)	

B. 빈칸에 알맞은 표현을 넣으시오.

based on (~에 근거하여)	instead of (~대신에)	in addition to (~에 더하여)
plenty of (많은)	In general (일반적으로)	

1. Activities should be chosen ( ) personal enjoyment and effectiveness.
2. ( ), exercise can help prevent diseases and reduce stress.
3. Cutting down on calories should be considered ( ) exercising.
4. Drink ( ) water before, during, and after exercising.
5. For example, ( ) using the stairs, people prefer to use elevators or escalators.

LET'S READ IT TOGETHER

Let's Work Out

1 Society is changing and more people do not want to do any kind of physical activity or exercise. For example, instead of using the stairs, people prefer to use elevators or escalators. But doctors say that we should get 30–60 minutes of physical activity everyday to be healthy. Doing simple exercises can improve energy levels and moods. But to really be healthy, it is more important to select the right type of exercise.

2 A well–balanced workout should include aerobic exercise, strength training, and flexibility training. Aerobic exercise can help build a strong heart by getting the heart pumping, which increases breathing and delivers more oxygen throughout the body. Running, cycling, swimming, and aerobic dance are some examples of aerobic exercise.

3 Strength training is also helpful and should be done for longer periods of time. Building strong muscles helps to protect the joints in the body and prevent injuries. There are various exercises that can be done to strengthen different muscle groups. For example, pull–ups and push–ups are good for the shoulders and chest. Squats and leg raises are good for the legs. Sit–ups and crunches are good for the abdominal muscles. It is a good idea to repeat the same exercises over and over again.

muscle

joint

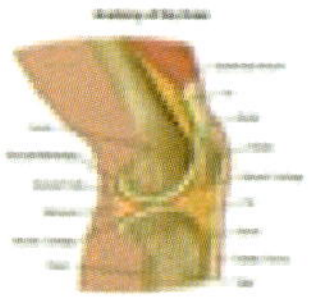

squat

Quick Comprehension Questions

1. How long should we do a physical activity everyday to be healthy?
2. What should a well–balanced work out include?
3. Which activities are good for building muscles in the shoulders and chest?

vocabulary

aerobic(유산소의) breathing(숨쉬기) oxygen(산소) pull–up(턱걸이)
chest(흉부) sit–up(윗몸 일으키기) crunch(윗몸 굽히기) abdominal(복부의)

4 Flexibility training involves bending and stretching to help keep the muscles flexible, which can help prevent injuries. Activities like stretching, gymnastics, and yoga are good choices for flexibility training. Drinking plenty of water before, during, and after exercising is important

5 For beginners, it is best to start by exercising three days a week for 20-30 minutes. Activities should be chosen based on personal enjoyment and effectiveness. Going to a health club is another great way to keep healthy. It can be a good choice for people who do not like to exercise alone and instead prefer being with someone. Also it is important to remember that for burning calories, walking and climbing stairs can be very effective as well as doing household chores.

6 So in general, exercise can help prevent diseases and reduce stress. It can also help us to look and feel better. And with exercise, a healthy diet should be followed as well, to reduce body fat and increase muscle mass. Therefore, for anyone wanting to lose weight, cutting down on calories should be considered in addition to exercising. So what are you waiting for? Let's work out!

abdominal

stairs

Quick Comprehension Questions

1. Which exercises are good examples for flexibility training?
2. Why can exercise be helpful?
3. To lose weight what should be done in addition to exercising?

vocabulary

bending(구부림. 굽힘) effectiveness(유효성) gymnastics(체조, 체조경기)
weight(체중) mass(질량) household(가정의) chore(잡일)

READING COMPREHENSION

A. Understanding the Main Idea: 본문의 요지로 알맞은 것을 고르시오.

1. Exercise is good for losing weight.
2. Exercise is good to maintain a healthy life.
3. We need to do the three types of strength training.
4. Beginners have to exercise everyday for 30 minutes.

B. Text Organization

박스 안에는 읽기 지문들의 주제들이 요약되어 있다. 아래 문장의 적절한 주제를 고르시오.

a. Aerobic exercise
b. Strength training
c. Flexibility training
d. How to start exercising
e. Advantage of exercise
f. What you need to do in addition to exercise.

____ 1. If you are a beginner, start by exercising three days a week for 20 to 30 minutes.
____ 2. It is any type of exercise that can help build a strong heart by getting the heart pumping.
____ 3. It helps make strong muscles that protect the joints in the body and prevent injuries.
____ 4. A healthy diet and cutting down on calories should be considered.
____ 5. It will also help your body improve flexibility.
____ 6. Exercise helps prevent disease and reduce stress.

C. Understanding Details:

아래의 문장이 본문의 내용과 맞으면 T, 틀리면 F를 선택하시오.

	True	False
1. Exercise increases body fat and reduces muscle mass.		
2. Climbing stairs is an example of a household chore.		
3. Sit-ups are a good exercise for the abdominals.		
4. Pull-ups are good for building chest muscles.		
5. Strong muscles improve flexibility.		
6. Aerobic exercise increases your breathing.		

D. Reading Strategy

훑어 읽기 와 찾아 읽기 (Skimming and Scanning)

훑어 읽기(skimming)는 요지 혹은 글의 구성을 파악하기 위해서 글 전체를 빠른 속도로 읽는 것을 말한다. 훑어 읽기는 글을 예측하거나 개략적으로 파악하는데 유용한 전략이다. 훑어 읽기를 할 때는 단어 하나하나 집중하지 말고 빠른 속도로 읽어 내려가며 소제목이나 단락의 첫 번째 문장 등에 주목한다.

찾아 읽기(scanning)는 특정 정보를 찾기 위해 글을 빨리 읽는 것을 말한다. 찾아 읽기는 핵심 개념의 정의, 구체적 정보 등을 찾는 데 다양하게 적용할 수 있으며 효율적 읽기를 위한 중요한 전략이다. 찾아 읽기를 할 대는 글 전체를 다 읽으려고 하지 말고 찾고자 하는 정보를 염두에 두고 빠른 속도로 읽어 나가야 한다.

Scanning Activity:

본문을 2분 동안 빨리 읽고 난 후 아래의 문단들을 한 문장으로 요약하시오

Read the text quickly within about 2 minutes and write a sentence summary for paragraphs below.

Paragraph 1:

____

Paragraph 2–4:

____

Paragraph 5:

____

VOCABULARY REVIEW

A. 빈칸에 알맞은 단어를 넣으시오.

prefer physical flexibility involve deliver injury strengthen burn

1. They didn't __________ the newspaper today.
2. Your son appears to be in good __________ health.
3. To improve __________ try to do a little stretching everyday.
4. I __________ beef to chicken
5. To be healthy will __________ healthy eating habits and regular exercise.
6. An __________ is damage to your body.
7. This exercise will __________ your neck.
8. Household chores can help you __________ calories.

B. Word Power

형용사+ –ity =명사

영어의 형용사에 접미사 '–ity'를 붙혀서 명사를 만든다. 형용사의 어휘가 모음으로 끝나는 경우는(예: flexible, able) 접미사의 모음과의 음운현상에 의해서 어휘 끝의 모음이 탈락되거나 변형되는 경우가 발생한다.

active (활동적인)+ ity ⇨ activity (활동)
flexible (유연한) + ity ⇨ flexibility (유연성)
real (진짜의) + ity ⇨ reality(현실)
able (가능한) + ity ⇨ ability(능력)
national (국가의) + ity ⇨ nationality (국적)

1. Camping is an interesting outdoor **activity** in summer.
2. Dancers need **flexibility**, so they stretch their bodies every day.
3. The house looks very old, but in **reality** it's quite new.
4. She has the **ability** to solve difficult math problems.

GRAMMAR FOCUS

Comparative (비교급)

비교급은 형용사의 1음절 단어에 -er을 붙인다. 1음절 단어의 경우 단모음+ 자음은 마지막 자음을 하나 더 쓰고 -er을 붙인다. y로 끝나는 형용사는 -y를 -i 로 바꾸고 -er을 붙인다. 2음절 이상의 형용사는 more를 형용사 앞에 쓴다. 형용사 뒤에 than을 쓰고 비교하는 대상을 쓴다.

Aerobic exercise can make your heart **stronger**.
It is **more important** to select the right type of exercise.
It can also help us to look and feel **better**.

규칙 형용사	불규칙 형용사
high - higher small - smaller hot - hotter easy - easier important - more important	good - better bad - worse little - less many - more far - farther / further

* 부록 참고

A. 빈칸에 적절한 어휘를 고르시오.

1. John is __________ than his brother. (handsome)
2. I'm tired and can't walk __________ than I am now. (fast)
3. Mary is __________ than her sister. (pretty)
4. The weather in August is __________ than the weather in June. (hot)

B. 다음 글을 읽고 틀린 부분을 찾아 맞게 고치시오.

Chris and his young brother John exercise every morning together. Usually, Chris runs long than his brother because he is big than him. But John can do many sit-ups and pull-ups than his brother because he is lean than Chris.

LET'S TALK ABOUT IT

A. 다음 대화를 듣고 연습해 봅시다.

Chris: Hi Minho. You look great! Are you working out these days?
Minho: Yeah. I exercise every morning for an hour.
Chris: Really? What do you do?
Minho: I go jogging and do weight training.
Chris: Wow, **I'd like to** work out too, but I can't find the time.
Minho: You can always try to make some time early in the morning.
Chris: You're right. I think I'm going to try that.
Minho: Just take it one step at a time.

B. 유용한 표현들

1. 무엇을 하고자 하는 표현을 사용할 때:

want to…, would like to..(..하고 싶다)등이 있고 be willing to.. (기꺼이 ..하다)와 같은 표현도 있다. Want 보다는 would like to가 더 정중한 표현이다.

I **would like to** have a great vacation.
I'**m willing to** cook dinner for you tonight.

2. 희망과 소원을 표현할 때

'..하기를 바란다/ 희망한다'의 뜻으로 hope와 wish가 있다. hope는 확실하지는 않지만 실현 가능성이 있는 소망을 말할 때 쓰고 wish는 대개 실현 불가능한 소망을 나타낸다.

I **hope** that you will be successful.
I **wish** that I didn't have to go. (안가도 된다면 좋을텐데)

* 현재나 미래의 실현가능성이 없는 일에 대한 바램을 나타내는 wish를 쓸 때는 that절의 동사는 과거형을 사용한다.

C. 말해보기: 아래 빈칸에 알맞은 표현을 넣으시오.

1. A: What are your plans for summer vacation? (너는 여름 방학 계획이 뭐니?)
   B: Well, I ___________ go on a trip to England.
   (음, 난 영국여행을 하고 싶어)

2. A: I have been waiting for her for three hours.
   (난 여기서 그녀를 세 시간동안 기다리고 있어)
   B: I ___________ she will come soon. (그녀가 곧 왔으면 좋겠다.)

COMMON ERRORS IN ENGLISH

Hiking vs. Mountain Climbing

Sujin: I go mountain climbing with my grandmother every Saturday.
Chris: Really? Wow, I'm impressed. Your grandmother must be very healthy and strong!
Sujin: Actually, not really. We just walk along the mountain paths.
Chris: Oh, you mean **hiking**! You should say, "I go hiking in the mountains with my grandmother every Saturday."

1. Hiking은 (시골이나 숲에서) 힘든 구간 없이 다듬어진 길을 따라 걷는 것을 의미한다.
   It's a perfect day for **hiking** and sightseeing.
   (도보여행하고 관광하기 완벽한 날이다.)

2. Mountain climbing 은 장비를 다 갖추고 하는 등산을 뜻한다
   June and July are good months for **mountain climbing** in Alaska.
   (6월과 7월은 알래스카 등산하기 좋은 달이다.)

Lesson 3
I DON'T KNOW WHAT TO WEAR

CONTENTS

WARM UP

A. 아래 그림을 보고 질문에 답하시오.

1. Which clothes do you think are out of date?
2. If you are male, which type of clothing would you prefer to wear?
3. If you are female, which style do you prefer to wear?

B. 대화를 듣고 질문에 답하시오.

Sujin: Do you like to wear stylish clothing?
Karen: No. But I like to wear anything that makes me look unique.
Sujin: I have a lot of clothes in my closet but there are only a few items I actually wear.
Karen: Oh, then it's time to update your clothing.
Sujin: How can I do that?
Karen: First, you need to get rid of clothing that is out of date.

1. What type of clothing does Karen like to wear?
2. Are there many things for Sujin to wear in her closet?
3. What does Sujin need to do to update her clothing?

vocabulary

a few (약간있는) few (거의 없는) update (갱신(업데이트)하다)

VOCABULARY PREVIEW

A. 단어의 뜻과 표현을 공부해 보세요.

1. comfort (편안, 안락)	a state of ease
find comfort in a mother's love (어머니의 사랑에 위안을 받다)	
2. outfit (옷, 복장)	a set or style of clothing
a sports outfit (스포츠 복장)	
3. lean (마른, 야윈)	having little fat on the body
This exercise will help you get a lean body. (이 운동은 몸을 날씬하게 하는데 도움이 된다.)	
4. organize (정리하다)	to arrange in an orderly way
It will help you organize your house. (그것은 집 정리를 하는데 도움이 될 것이다.)	
5. current (현재의)	recent times
current events (시사 (현재 사건들))	
6. appear (…처럼 보이다)	to seem or look like something
Things are not always as they appear. (일들이 항상 보이 것과 같지는 않다.)	
7. fit (..에 꼭 맞다)	to be the proper size, shape, etc
This suit fits. (이 정장은 (몸에) 딱 맞다.)	
8. favorite (특히 좋아하는 것)	person or thing someone likes the best
a list of my favorites (내가 좋아하는 것들의 목록)	
9. stylish (멋진)	using current styles in clothing
That's a stylish outfit. (그것은 멋진 복장이다.)	
10. match (어울리다)	to suit or fit (one thing) to another
Do these colors match? (이 색들이 (서로) 어울리니?)	

B. 빈칸에 알맞은 표현을 넣으시오.

find out (알아 보다, 찾아보다)	get rid of (제거하다)	out of date (구식의)
looks good on (보기 좋은)	according to (~에 의하면)	

1. Get rid of clothing that is ( ).
2. This coat ( ) you.
3. Buy clothes ( ) your body shape and size.
4. Let's ( ) what interesting books are in the library.
5. ( ) what clothes you don't like in your closet.

LET'S READ IT TOGETHER

I don't know what to wear

1 Do you like to go clothes shopping? Clothes are important for protection as well as comfort. Do you like to wear stylish clothes or is comfort more important? What we wear often says a lot about who we are and what we are feeling to others around us.

2 When preparing what to wear, here are some things to think about to help you feel comfortable and look your best. First, know your body type and what kinds of clothing are well fitted for you. Second, put some thought into your choices because what you wear often affects how others view you, and how you feel about yourself. Third, know what the current fashion trends are, and decide what to keep and update in your wardrobe.

3 How do you know it's time to update your clothing? Check if you have clothing in your closet that you bought 10 or more years ago. Unless these are your favorite, it's time to organize your closet. Then, think carefully about the styles you love. This is the start of improving your personal image. Next, consider what types of clothing you feel comfortable wearing and what kinds of outfits make you look great. Finally, get rid of clothing that is out of date or no longer fits you or your lifestyle.

wardrobe

closet

Quick Comprehension Questions

1. Why are clothes important to us?
2. What is the first step of knowing what clothes to wear?
3. What is the first step to update your clothing?

vocabulary

protection(보호) comfortable(편안한) prepare(준비하다) clothing(의류)
clothes(옷) trend(유행) personal(개인적인)

4 Color is something else to think about because it plays a big part in your image. Find what colors look good on you and build your wardrobe around them. This will help you mix and match your clothes selection. After this, try clothing items in new combinations to find items that work well together. You should also find out what you need and then go shopping for them. Remember to buy clothes according to your body shape and size. For example, when choosing styles, avoid horizontal stripes that can make you appear wide or heavy, and instead, consider vertical stripes which make you look taller and leaner.

Horizontal

vertical

5 Finally, if you're working, you need to dress appropriately. Black is basic for office workers. As an alternative, gray, navy blue, or other dark colors are fine. Whatever you wear, be sure it says something about you and the image you would like others to see. What you wear is a chance to let others know a little about you. So as a general rule, "dress to impress."

Quick Comprehension Questions

1. Which type of style makes you look taller?
2. Why are colors important in choosing clothes?
3. What is a general rule for choosing clothing?

vocabulary

item(품목) avoid(피하다) stripe(줄무늬) instead(대신에) combination(배합) appropriately(상황에 어울리게) alternative(대안) impress(깊은 인상을 주다)

READING COMPREHENSION

A. Understanding the Main Idea: 본문의 요지로 알맞은 것을 고르시오.

1. Choosing a good job outfit will change your lifestyle.
2. Clothes tell you about you and your lifestyle.
3. Choosing colors is important in making your personal image.
4. You need to update your clothing to be stylish.

B. Text Organization

박스 안에는 읽기 지문들의 주제들이 요약되어 있다.아래 문장의 적절한 주제를 고르시오.

a. The essential parts of knowing what to wear
b. How to update your clothing
c. Choosing colors
d. Choosing a work outfit

____ 1. Find what colors look good on you and build your wardrobe around them.
____ 2. It's time to organize your closet. Think carefully about the styles you love.
____ 3. Black is basic for office workers.
____ 4. First, know your body type and what kinds of clothing are well fitted for you.

C. Understanding Details:

아래의 문장이 본문의 내용과 맞으면 T, 틀리면 F를 선택하시오.

	True	False
1. You have to know your body type to dress with style.		
2. If you want to look heavy, consider vertical stripes.		
3. When you go shopping for clothes, knowing your body shape and size is important.		
4. Finding out your style is important in creating your personal image.		
5. You can wear any comfortable style if you are an office worker.		
6. Color plays a big part in your personal image.		

D. Reading Strategy

과정/절차 파악하기 (Understanding Process)

"~을/를 하는 과정 또는 절차"를 설명하는 글을 읽을 때에 독자는 각 단계에서 설명되는 내용을 명확히 파악하는 것이 중요하다. 이러한 글에는 절차의 순서를 표시하는 다음과 같은 어구들이 나타난다.

– first (of all), second, next, then, lastly, finally

아래 문장들을 순서대로 나열하시오. 빈칸에 순서대로 번호를 넣으시오.

a. Know your body type before you update your clothes.
b. Find out what you need and then go shopping for them.
c. Check your clothes to find out what styles you love.
d. There are steps for choosing the right clothes.
e. Find items in your closet that work well together.

1. First, ____________________
2. Second, ____________________
3. Next, ____________________
4. After that, ____________________
5. Finally, ____________________

VOCABULARY REVIEW

A. 빈칸에 알맞은 단어를 넣으시오.

stylish opportunities fit current favorite organize match appears

1. The blue suit is my __________.
2. You look very __________ in that red dress.
3. He __________ to be a successful man.
4. The pants __________ me very well.
5. Traveling provides __________ to experience other cultures.
6. The shoes __________ this dress.
7. Studying hard will help you pick out the main points and __________ them.
8. I read the newspaper to learn about __________ events in the world.

B. Word Power

동사 + –able = 형용사

> 영어의 동사에 접미사 '–able'를 붙혀서 형용사를 만든다. 동사가 모음으로 끝나는 경우는(예: value) 접미사의 모음과의 음운현상에 의해서 어휘 끝의 모음이 탈락되거나 변형되는 경우가 발생한다.

comfort (편하게하다)+ able ⇨ comfortable (편안한)
enjoy (즐기다)+ able ⇨ enjoyable (즐거운)
accept (받아들이다) + able ⇨ acceptable (받아들일 수 있는)
value (중요시하다) + able ⇨ valuable (귀중한, 값이 나가는)

1. This chair is very **comfortable**.
2. We had an **enjoyable** time with his family.
3. Casual clothes are **acceptable** in our office.
4. This is a **valuable** book. Don't throw it away.

GRAMMAR FOCUS

Relative Pronoun (주격 관계대명사)

주격 관계대명사는 who, which, that 이 있다. Who는 선행사가 사람이고 주어인 (대)명사 대신에 쓰인다. Which는 선행사가 사물이나 동물이고 주어인 명사 대신에 쓴다. That은 who와 which대신에 쓸 수 있다. 관계대명사가 이끄는 형용사절의 동사는 선행사에 의해 결정된다.

Consider vertical stripes **which** make you look taller and leaner.
Get rid of clothing **that** is out of date and no longer fits you and your lifestyle.
He is the man **who** helped me yesterday.

Who	Which
I like the woman. She lives next to me. ⇨ I like the woman **who** lives next to me. ⇨ I like the woman **that** lives next to me	The library is good. It is near my house. ⇨ The library **which** is near my house is good. ⇨ The library **that** is near my house is good

A. 아래 빈칸에 알맞은 주격 관계대명사를 넣으시오.

1. The person ___________ is sitting in front of me is very noisy.
2. Find the items in your closet ___________ work well together.
3. This is the bag ___________ I bought in America.
4. I thanked the man ___________ helped me.

B. 다음 글을 읽고 틀린 부분을 찾아 맞게 고치시오.

If you are a person which wants to dress with style, you need to know your body type. To follow current fashion trends, you need to get rid of clothing who is out of date. After that, try to find colors who look good on you.

LET'S TALK ABOUT IT

A. 다음 대화를 듣고 연습해 봅시다.

Sujin: I don't know what to wear to the party this weekend.
Karen: Just wear something casual.
Sujin: But I only have suits.
Karen: You mean you don't have any casual clothes?
Sujin: I have some, but they're old fashioned.
Karen: Then **let's go** shopping for a new outfit. I'll help you choose.
Sujin: That would be great! Thanks.

B. 유용한 표현들

1. 상대방에게 무엇을 제안하거나 권유할 때:

Why don't you..? (..하는게 어때요?) , What about.. , How about ..., (… 는 어때요?), You'd better +동사원형(..하는게 낫겠다)와 같은 표현이 있다. 좀 더 정중한 표현으로는 Would you like to…(..하시겠어요?)를 사용한다.

What about (how about) a nice scarf?
(좋은 스카프는 어때? (선물을 사는 것에 대한 제안))
You'd better quit smoking. (담배를 끊는 것이 좋겠다.)

2. 함께 어떤 것을 하자고 제안하는 경우:

Let' + 동사원형…(….합시다) 를 쓴다. 의문문의 형태로 사용할 때는 Why don't we..?, 나 Shall we..? (… 할까요?)를 사용한다.

Why don't we stay a little longer? (우리 조금 더 체류하는 것이 어떨까?)

C. 말해보기: 아래 빈칸에 알맞은 표현을 넣으시오.

A: ___________ visiting your brother? (너의 형을 방문하는 것이 어떠니?)
B: Ok. (그래)

A: ___________ go to America this summer. (우리 이번 여름에 미국에 가도록 하자.)
B: That sounds good. (그것 좋겠다.)

Cloths vs. Clothes

Sujin: Karen has nice cloths. She always wears fashionable cloths.
Chris: Uh,... **cloth** is what is used to make clothing or a piece of cloth can be used for cleaning something, like wiping a table. So to say 'she has nice cloths' sounds strange.
Sujin: Oh, what I mean is she wears beautiful things like skirts, blouses, and jackets.
Chris: Right, then you should say, '**clothes**' or 'clothing', not 'cloths'.

1. Cloth는 '옷감, 직물'을 의미한다. 천으로 만든 '헝겊, 수건, 걸레'를 말할 때 사용한다.

   Please wipe the floor with a wet **cloth**.
   (마루를 젖은 걸레로 닦아주세요.)
   I want to buy this round, white **tablecloth**.
   (나는 이 흰색 둥근 식탁보를 사고 싶어요.)

2. Clothes는 '옷, 의복'을 뜻하는 명사이다. Clothing은 '의류, 복장'을 뜻하는 말로 신체를 감싸는 의복 전반의 총칭으로 쓰인다.

   I like fashionable **clothes**.
   (나는 유행하는 옷을 좋아해요)
   Women's clothing (여성의류)　Protective clothing (보호복)

Lesson 4
AN AMERICAN WHO WAS MORE KOREAN THAN KOREANS

CONTENTS

Reading: 한국을 사랑한 미국인에 관한 이야기

Reading Strategy: 이야기의 전개 순서 파악하기

Word Power: 나라와 관계된 단어들

Grammar Focus: 단순과거

Let's Talk About It: 과거에 한 일

Common Errors in English: Trip vs. Take a trip

WARM UP

A. 아래 그림을 보고 질문에 답하시오

1. What do these three people have in common?
2. What are their Korean names ?
3. What are their jobs?

B. 대화를 듣고 질문에 답하시오

Chris: I'm going to travel to Taean this weekend. What should I see there, Sujin?
Sujin: You should visit the Chollipo Arboretum, Chris.
Chris: What is it famous for?
Sujin: It is one of the most beautiful gardens in the world.
Chris: It's amazing. Do you know who made it?
Sujin: Yeah, a man named Min Byng-gal did.
Chris: Min Byng-gal? I've never heard such a strange Korean name.

1. Chris is going to Taean next weekend. T F
2. The Chollipo Arboretum is a kind of garden. T F
3. A man named Min Byung-gal made the Chollipo Arboretum. T F

vocabulary

What is it famous for? (그것은 뭐로 유명하니?)
one of the most ~ (가장 ~한 것들 중 하나) It's amazing
A man named ~ (~라는 이름의 남자)
I've never heard ~ (~을 들어 본 적이 없다)
such a strange Korean name (그렇게 이상한 한국 이름)

VOCABULARY PREVIEW

A. 단어의 뜻과 표현을 공부해 보시오.

1. raise (기르다) to make an animal or plant grow
We raised a cow. (우리는 소를 키웠다.)

2. establish (설립하다) to start a company or organization
He established a school. (그는 학교를 설립했다.)

3. preserve (보존하다) to keep something the same
We should preserve our culture. (우리 문화를 보존해야 한다)

4. rare (희귀한) very unusual
Gold is very rare. (금은 매우 귀하다)

5. anxious (열망하는) wanting to do something
They are anxious to learn new things. (그들은 새로운 것을 배우길 열망한다.)

6. valuable (가치 있는) having worth
Her advice was valuable to me. (그녀의 조언은 내게 소중했다.)

7. entire (전체의) whole or complete
I spent an entire day on it. (나는 하루 종일 그것을 했다.)

8. wander (방황하다) to walk slowly about a place
We wandered around the street. (우리는 거리를 헤매 다녔다.)

9. award (상을 주다) to give someone a prize officially
He was awarded a scholarship. (그는 장학금을 받았다.)

10. environment (환경) things around people in their life
The environment in big cities is usually polluted. (대도시의 환경은 대개 오염되어 있다.)

B. 빈칸에 알맞은 표현을 넣으시오.

became interested in,	happened to,	died of,	fell in love with,	is full of
(~에 관심이 생기다)	(~우연히 하다)	(~로 죽다)	(~와 사랑에 빠지다)	(~로 가득 찬)

1. The garden ( ) various kinds of flowers and trees.
2. Carl Miller ( ) the landscape of Korea.
3. Carl Miller ( ) meet some Buddhist monks.
4. Carl Miller ( ) raising Korean flowers and trees.
5. The man ( ) cancer at the age of 82.

LET'S READ IT TOGETHER

An American who was more Korean than Koreans

1 The Chollipo Arboretum in Taean, South Chungcheong Province is known as one of the most beautiful gardens in the world. It is full of various kinds of rare and exotic flowers and trees. Surprisingly, this scenic environment that is so valuable in Korea was built by an American who lived in Korea for 57 years.

2 Carl Ferris Miller was born in Pennsylvania, U.S.A. in 1921. He came to Korea in 1945 as a member of the U.S. Navy. Soon afterward, he fell in love with the landscape of Korea. In 1952, he left the navy and got a job at the Bank of Korea. Every weekend, he went hiking in the mountains. One day, he happened to meet some Buddhist monks and learned about Korean plants. After that, he became interested in raising Korean flowers and trees.

3 In 1962, Miller first visited Chollipo and bought some land to build a garden. Over the next 30 years, he spent his entire time and money caring for the garden. He wandered the mountains and fields to collect wild herbs and flowers. He also brought in seeds of new species from foreign countries. The garden grew bigger and bigger, and Miller finally established the Chollipo Arboretum in 1979.

arboretum

Buddhist monk

navy

Quick Comprehension Questions

1. Where is the Chollipo Arboretum located?
2. What did Miller do every weekend?
3. When did Miller get a job at the Bank of Korea?

vocabulary

various (다양한) natural(자연적인) build(건설하다) afterward (나중에)
collect(채집하다) plant(식물) species((식물이나 동물의)종)

4 Before long, the Chollipo Arboretum became famous worldwide. In 2000, it was awarded the "Arboretum Distinguished for Merit", which was the first in Asia. As a result, people became anxious to visit the Arboretum, but Miller did not open it to the public because he wanted to preserve and protect it

5 In many ways, Miller was more Korean than Koreans. When asked about his love for Korea, he is quoted as saying, "Maybe, I was a Korean in a previous life." He lived in a hanok and enjoyed wearing hanbok and eating kimchi. He eventually became a Korean citizen in 1979 and even made a Korean name, Min, Byung-Gal. He died of cancer in 2002 at the age of 81.

6 Currently, the Chollipo Arboretum is open to the public. There are about 7,000 kinds of plants represented from Korea and abroad at the arboretum. Every year, thousands of people visit there and enjoy its natural beauty, which is the result of Min, Byung-Gal's life-long love and devotion to the country he called home.

herb

seed

Quick Comprehension Questions

1. When was the Chollipo Arboretum awarded the "Arboretum Distinguished for Merit"?
2. What is Miller's Korean name?
3. Why didn't Miller open the Arboretum to the public?

vocabulary

finally(마침내) worldwide(전세계적으로) public(공공의) quote(인용하다)
previous(과거) eventually(궁극적으로) currently(현재) devotion(헌신)

READING COMPREHENSION

A. Understanding the Main Idea: 본문의 요지로 알맞은 것을 고르시오.

1. Establishment of the Cheollipo Arboretum by Carl Miller.
2. Rare and exotic flowers and trees in the Cheollipo Arboretum.
3. Min Byung-gal's devotion to the Cheollipo Arboretum.
4. Natural beauty of the Cheollipo Arboretum.

B. Text Organization

아래에 제시된 일들을 일어난 시간 순서대로 배열하여 표를 완성하시오

Events	a. Miller first visited Chollipo. b. The Chollipo Arboretum was awarded "Arboretum Distinguished for Merit." c. The Chollipo Arboretum was established. d. Miller got a job at the Bank of Korea. e. Miller came to Korea as a member of the U.S. navy. f. Miller became a Korean citizen and made a Korean name.
1945	
1952	
1962	
1979	
2000	

C. Understanding Details:
아래의 문장이 본문의 내용과 맞으면 T, 틀리면 F를 선택하시오.

	True	False
1. The Chollipo Arboretum is known as one of the most beautiful gardens in Asia.		
2. Miller served for the U.S. army during World War II.		
3. There are only Korean flowers and trees in the Chollipo Arboretum.		
4. Miller lived in Korea in a previous life.		
5. Miller opened the Chollipo Arboretum to the public to make money.		
6. Miller lived in hanok and enjoyed wearing habok.		

D. Reading Strategy

이야기속의 사건 전개 순서 파악하기 (Understanding Sequence of Events)

소설 등의 이야기에서는 사건이 일어난 때나 순서에 따라 사건이 진행된다. 사건의 진행 순서를 나타내는 표현들(after, before, first, finally, immediately, next, now, soon, then, today, until)이 많이 사용된다. 이러한 표현들에 유의하면서 사건의 흐름을 순서대로 파악하면 이야기의 전개과정을 더 명확하게 이해할 수 있다.

아래 주어진 사건들이 일어난 순서대로 문장 앞에 번호를 매겨 보시오.

_1_ Carl Miller was born in Pennsylvania, U.S.A. in 1921.
___ One day, he learned about Korean plants from some Buddhist monks.
___ After that, he became interested in raising Korean flowers and trees.
___ He arrived in Korea in 1945 as a member of the U.S. Navy.
___ 7 years later, he got a job at the Bank of Korea.
___ Soon afterward, he fell in love with the landscape of Korea.

VOCABULARY REVIEW

A. 빈칸에 알맞은 단어를 넣으시오.

raise establish valuable preserve rare environment award anxious

1. The boy did not win the race, but he learned a ___________ lesson from the experience.
2. The new bridge may cause damage to the ___________.
3. Before the printing machine was invented, books were ___________.
4. My father has a big farm where he ___________ a lot of cows.
5. President Kim Dae-jung was ___________ the Nobel Peace Prize in 2000.
6. Many people fight to ___________ the world's natural beauty and resources.
7. A lot of Koreans are ___________ to speak English well.
8. The United Nation was ___________ in October 1945.

B. Word Power

나라와 관련된 단어들

나라를 뜻하는 명사는 다양한 방식으로 변형되어 해당나라를 뜻하는 형용사, 국적, 언어를 표현한다.

Country	Adjective	Nationality	Language
Korea	Korean	Korean	Korean
Italy	Italian	Italian	Italian
Japan	Japanese	Japanese	Japanese
France	French	French	French
England	English	English	English
United States	American	American	English

1. Where are you from? What's your nationality? (X)
   Where do you come from? I'm from **Korea**.
2. A: Which food do you like best? B: I like **Italian** food.
3. A: Are you **Japanese**? B: No, I'm **Chinese**.
4. A: Can you speak **French**? B: No, I can't, but I can speak **Spanish**.

참고: 미국인들은 국적을 묻는 질문에 "I'm American."이라고 답하는 데 America 대륙의 다른 나라 사람들은 미국인을 North American이라고 부르는 경향이 있다.

GRAMMAR FOCUS

Simple past (단순과거)

동사의 단순 과거형은 과거에 일어난 사건, 행동 혹은 과거의 습관 등에 대해 말할 때 사용된다. 주로 동사 원형에 -ed를 붙여 만들지만 불규칙한 형태도 있다. 과거를 표현하는 말들(last year, yesterday, 10 years ago, in 2000)에 주의해서 동사의 형태를 맞춰 써야 한다.

Miller first **visited** Chollipo in 1962.
He **came** to Korea 65 years ago.
He **dies** of cancer in 2002 at the age of 81.(**X**)
⇨ He **died** of cancer in 2002 at the age of 81.(**O**)

Regular verbs		Irregular verbs	
live-live**d**	stay-stay**ed**	build-**built**	find-**found**
use-use**d**	study-studi**ed**	know-**knew**	see-**saw**

Present	fall	go	become	buy	say	get	eat
Past							

* 부록 참고

A. 알맞은 동사의 과거형을 선택하여 문장을 완성하시오.

1. He (becomed/became) famous.
2. My mother (falled/fell) on the street last week.
3. He (builded/built) a new house.
4. I (getted/got) up late this morning

B. 다음 글을 읽고 틀린 부분을 찾아 맞게 고치시오.

Yesterday, I go to Lotte Department with my sister. At the clothing section, my sister buy a skirt, and then we see a new Spielberg movie, which is very fun. After the movie, we go to Starbucks. We drink coffee and eat some sandwiches. On our way home, my sister say, "it is a great day."

LET'S TALK ABOUT IT

A. 다음 대화를 듣고 연습해 봅시다

Minho: Hi, Karen. **Did you do anything special during the weekend?**
Karen: **Nothing special**. I just stayed home all day. **What did you do**, Minho?
Minho: I went to Seoul Grand Park with my girl friend.
Karen: **How was it?**
Minho: **It was terrible**. There were so many people there. We didn't get to see much.
Karen: That's too bad.

B. 유용한 표현들

1. 과거에 뭘 했는지 묻고 답할 때 일반적으로 **What did you do** (last weekend, yesterday..)?라고 하지만 **Did you do anything special during the weekend?**라고 묻기도 한다. 대답할 때의 표현은 다음과 같다.
    - 구체적으로 한 일이 있으면: I played tennis. I went shopping with my wife.
    - 별일 없었으면: Nothing special. Nothing much.

2. 과거에 한 일이 어땠는지에 대한 질문(**How was it? How was everything?**)에 대한 답은
    - 좋았을 때: **It was good**. 아주 좋았을 때: **It was great**. **It was wonderful**.
      미국 젊은이들은 **It was awesome**(굉장했어)이라는 표현도 많이 한다.
    - 나빴을 때: It was bad. 아주 나빴을 때는 **It was terrible**(형편없었어).

C. 말해보기: 아래 빈칸에 알맞은 표현을 넣으시오.

1. A: Did you do anything special during the vacation? (휴가 동안 뭐 특별한 일 했어?)
   B: ______________. I just watched TV all day. (별일 없었어. 종일 TV만 봤어)

2. A: How was your trip? (여행 어땠어?)
   B: ______________. We had a really good time. (굉장했어. 정말 재미있게 보냈어)

COMMON ERRORS IN ENGLISH

Trip vs. Take a trip

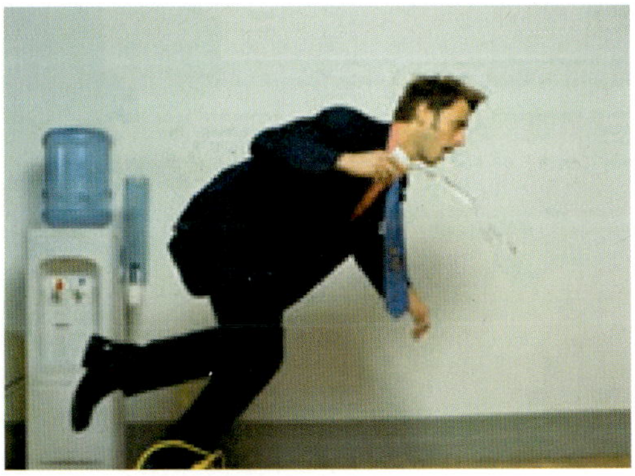

Sujin: Chris, we are going to **trip** to Busan this week.
Chris: Pardon? Sujin. You mean you are going to **take a trip** to Busan?
Sujin: Well… Yes, we are going to take a trip to Busan.
Chris: Ok, that sounds much better.

1. trip은 짧은 여행을 뜻하는 말로 명사로만 사용된다.
- Do you need help planning **your trip** to Paris? (파리로 여행 준비하는데 도움이 필요하니?)
- I'm **on a business trip** now.(나는 출장 중이다)

2. 여행가다라고 말하고 싶으면 take a trip이나 go on a trip이라고 말해야 한다. 여행을 자주 가는 경우는 take trips 또는 go on trips라고 말하면 된다.
- We **took a trip** to New York last year. (작년에 뉴욕으로 여행 갔다)
- He is **going on a trip**. (그는 여행 중이야)
- Jason ofen **takes trips** to Europe. (제이슨은 유럽으로 자주 여행 간다.)

3. To trip이 동사로 쓰이면 여행이라는 뜻이 아니라 "-을 헛딛어 넘어지다"나 "-에 걸려 넘어지다"라는 뜻이 된다.
- My daughter **tripped** and fell. (내 딸이 발을 헛디뎌 넘어졌다).
- Be careful not to **trip** up on the step. (계단에서 발을 헛디디지 않게 조심해라).

Lesson 5

A CHEROKEE WOMAN WHO MADE A DIFFERENCE

CONTENTS

Reading: 체로키 부족을 부흥시킨 여성 추장 이야기

Reading Strategy: 인과 관계 파악하기

Word Power: (un, im, il)+형용사

Grammar Focus: 시간을 표현하는 전치사

Let's Talk About It: 자유시간에 하는 일에 대해 추천하고 답하기

Common Errors in English: Keep health vs Stay healthy

WARM UP

A. 아래 그림을 보고 질문에 답하시오.

Margaret Datcher

Aungsan Suu kyi

Hillery Clinton

1. What do you think the women in the pictures have in common?
2. What countries are they from?
3. What are their achievements?

B. 대화를 듣고 질문에 답하시오.

Chris: Hey Minho, what are you doing?
Minho: Oh hey Chris, I'm reading the newspaper. There's a very interesting article about a female Native American chief.
Chris: Oh! You mean Wilma Mankiller?
Minho: Yeah, How did you hear about her?
Chris: She was a great leader. I learned about her in my American History class. She passed away a few weeks ago.
Minho: Wow, I didn't know she was such a historic figure.

1. Wilma Makiller was an American history teacher. T F
2. Chris learned about Wilma Mankiller in his American history class. T F
3. Wilma Mankiller is alive. T F

vocabulary

female (여성) article (신문기사) Native American (미국 인디언을 부르는 말)
chief (추장) leader (지도자) American History (미국역사)
pass away (돌아가다 (die (죽다)보다는 좀 더 간접적 표현))
historic figure (역사적인 인물)

VOCABULARY PREVIEW

A. 단어의 뜻과 표현을 공부해 보세요.

1. mourn (애도하다) — to feel sad about someone's death
The whole world mourn his death. (전 세계가 그의 죽음을 애도한다.)

2. occupy (점거하다) — to move in and take control of a place
Few of the tables are occupied. (몇 테이블에만 사람이 앉아있다.)

3. protest (항의하다) — to speak strongly against
Earth Day began as a protest. (지구의 날은 항의운동에서 시작되었다.)

4. progress (진보) — improvement of skills or knowledge
The country is slow in progress. (그 나라는 진보속도가 느리다)

5. overcome (극복하다) — to control a problem or feeling
I am trying to overcome my weakness. (나는 약점을 극복하려고 노력 중이다.)

6. population (인구) — the number of people in an area
The population is about nineteen million. (인구는 약 1천 9백만 명이다.)

7. government (정부) — a group of people who control a country
It is subsidized by the government. (정부로부터 보조금을 받는다.)

8. remember (기억하다) — to keep something in your memory
I can't remember who she is. (나는 그녀가 누군지 기억할 수 없다.)

9. injure (부상당하다) — to hurt a part of your body
Does athletics injure health? (운동은 건강을 상하게 하는가?)

10. threaten (협박하다) — to say that you will kill or hurt someone
He tried to threaten me. (그는 나를 협박하려 했다.)

B. 빈칸에 알맞은 표현을 넣으시오.

made fun of,	suffered from,	participated in,	played an important role in,	ran for
(놀리다)	(고통을 겪다)	(참여하다)	(-에 중요한 역할을 하다)	(출마하다)

1. These experiences ( ) her life.
2. Wilma heard about the news and ( ) the protest.
3. She ( ) the Principal Chief of the Cherokee Nation.
4. She also ( ) cancer.
5. Her classmates, mostly Whites, ( ) her.

LET'S READ IT TOGETHER

A Cherokee Woman Who Made a Difference

1 A Cherokee woman named Wilma Mankiller died of cancer at age 64 on April 6, 2010. Many Americans were deeply saddened to hear the news. Even President Obama expressed his sadness about her death. What made so many people mourn the death of this woman?

2 Wilma Mankiller was born in the small town of Tahlequah, Oklahoma in 1945. Her name, Mankiller, comes from her great great grandfather and is a translation of the Cherokee language meaning a warrior who protects Cherokee villages. Her family was poor and lived without electricity or indoor plumbing. However, Mankiller was happy. She enjoyed reading books and playing with other Cherokee children.

3 Her life changed suddenly when she was 12. Her family had to move because the U.S. government relocated Native American families like hers in order to make room for a military base. Mankiller and her family moved to San Francisco where she entered junior high school. However, her school life was not a happy one because her classmates, mostly Whites, made fun of her last name and her being Native Amercian.

4 These school experiences played an important role in Mankiller joining the Cherokee civil rights movement. In 1969, a group of Native American students occupied the former Alcatraz Prison, on Alcatraz Island located in San Francisco Bay, to protest against unfair treatment of the Native American people by the U.S. government. Mankiller heard about the news and participated in the protest. After this experience, she decided to dedicate her life to improving the welfare of the Cherokee people. She moved back to Oklahoma in 1977.

warrior

electricity

indoor plumbing

Quick Comprehension Questions

1. Where was Mankiller born?
2. When did she move to San Francisco?
3. Why did Native American students occupy Alcatraz?

vocabulary

deep(깊은) sadness(슬픔) move(이사가다) relocate(재배치하다) experience(경험) against(-에 반대하여) unfair(부당한) treatment(대우) welfare(복지)

5 In Oklahoma, Mankiller worked hard to help the Cherokee people improve their living conditions. As a result, new water systems were created and the old houses were rebuilt. Soon after, her success stories became known all over the country and she became famous.

6 Despite her success, she experienced many hardships. She was seriously injured in a car accident in 1979, and also suffered from cancer. But Mankiller overcame these challenges and ran for the position of Principal Chief of the Cherokee Nation in 1985. However, many Cherokee people did not want her to be their leader just because she was a woman. Some even threatened her life. Despite the challenges, she became the first female chief in the history of the Cherokee Nation.

7 After Mankiller took office as Principal Chief, the Cherokee Nation made great progress. The population increased, more people got jobs, and many new health centers and children's programs were established. She also worked hard to preserve the Cherokee language and traditions. She is now remembered as a great leader who made a difference in lives of the Native American people.

principal chief

health center

Quick Comprehension Questions

1. What happened to Mankiller in 1979?
2. When did she run for the Principal Chief of the Cherokee Nation?
3. Why didn't many Cherokee people want Mankiller to be their chief?

vocabulary

success(성공) hardship(어려움) seriously(심각하게) challenge(도전)
despite(-에도 불구하고) female(여성) tradition(전통)

READING COMPREHENSION

A. Understanding the Main Idea: 본문의 요지로 알맞은 것을 고르시오.

1. Sadness about Wilma Mankiller's death
2. Achievements of Wilma Makiller as Indian chief
3. The death of a Cherokee woman
4. The tradition of Cherokee Indians

B. Text Organization

다음에 주어진 주제를 다루고 있는 문단을 찾아 연결하시오.

Para 1 •	• a. Becoming the first female Principal Chief.
Para 2 •	• b. Experiences in a big city
Para 3 •	• c. Becoming famous nationwide
Para 4 •	• d. Death of the great female Cherokee chief
Para 5 •	• e. Achievements of Wilma as a Principal Chief
Para 6 •	• f. Joining Cherokee Indian rights movement.
Para 7 •	• g. Early years in hometown

C. Understanding Details:
아래의 문장이 본문의 내용과 맞으면 T, 틀리면 F를 선택하시오.

	True	False
1. Her name, Mankiller, means a warrior who kills men.		
2. Her family moved to San Francisco because they wanted to live in a big city.		
3. Some Native American students occupied an island near San Francisco for one year.		
4. Wilma was seriously injured in a car accident in 1979.		
5. Wilma was the first female chief in the Cherokee history.		
6. After Wilma became the Principal Chief, some Cherokees threatened to kill her.		

D. Reading Strategy

인과 관계 파악하기(Understanding Cause and Effect)

A 로 인해 B 가 일어나는 인과 관계를 기술한 글에서는 어떤 사건의 원인과 결과를 논리적으로 파악하는 것이 중요합니다. 인과 관계를 나타내기 위해 자주 쓰이는 표현들 (**because, so, then, therefore, as a result**) 에 특히 유의하면서 중심이 되는 사건이 어떻게 전개되는지에 초점을 맞추어 순차적인 인과 관계의 흐름을 파악해 봅시다. 인과 관계를 나타내는 글에서는 아래의 예에서처럼 원인이 주로 앞에 오는 경우가 많습니다.

- Jason worked hard, so he became rich.
  원인 ⟹ **결과**
- Because Jason worked hard, he became rich.
- Jason worked hard. As a result, he became rich.

그러나 다음 문장을 보면 결과가 먼저 나오고 그 뒤에 원인이 제시 된다.

- Jason became rich because he worked hard.
  결과 ⟸ **원인**

따라서 원인이 되는 내용이 항상 앞에 오는 것이 아니라 문장들간의 의미 관계에 따라 인과관계를 파악해야 합니다.

이탤릭 체로 씌어 있는 부분의 원인이 되는 문장을 찾아 밑줄을 쳐 보시오.

Wilma decided to live for the Cherokee people, so she moved back to Oklahoma in 1977. She worked hard to help the Cherokee people improve their living conditions. As a result, ***new water systems were created and the old houses were rebuilt***. Soon after, her success stories became known all over the country and she became famous.

Wilma moved back to Oklahoma in 1977 because she decided to live for the Cherokee people. She worked hard to help the Cherokee people improve their living conditions. As a result, new water systems were created and the old houses were rebuilt. Soon after, her success stories became known all over the country and she became famous.

VOCABULARY REVIEW

A. 빈칸에 알맞은 단어를 넣으시오.

mourns	government	progress	protesting
remember	injured	overcome	population

1. What's the (   ) of Korea?
2. A group of students are (   ) against the tuition increase.
3. My daughter made a great (   ) in English last year.
4. You should (   ) your shyness in class to be fluent in English.
5. My mother (   ) her back when she fell.
6. I can't (   ) where I parked my car.
7. He (   ) for his dead brother every day.
8. The Korean (   ) was established on Aug. 15, 1948

B. Word Power

형용사의 반의어: un (im or il) + 형용사

영어의 형용사 앞에 접두사를 붙여 반의어를 만들 수 있는 경우가 많다. 'un'이 가장 흔하게 쓰이고 'im' 또는 'il'을 붙이는 경우도 있다. 어떤 단어에 어떤 접두사를 붙이면 반의어가 되는 지 정확히 알면 어휘력을 높이는 데 대단히 효과적이다.

fair(공정한) ⇨ **un**fair(불공정한)
usual(흔한) ⇨ **un**usual(흔치 않은)
perfect(완전한) ⇨ **im**perfect(불완전한)
legal(합법적인) ⇨ **il**legal(불법인)
happy(행복한) ⇨ **un**happy(불행한)
able(할 능력 있는) ⇨ **un**able(할 능력 없는)
possible(가능한) ⇨ **im**possible(불가능한)
logical(논리적인) ⇨ **il**logical(비논리적인)

1. Most workers felt the decision was **unfair**.
2. Jason was **unhappy**, but he still smiled.
3. The question was very difficult, so I was **unable** to answer it.
4. Some people think it is **impolite** to ask someone's age.
5. Smoking in public is **illegal** in some countries.

GRAMMAR FOCUS

시간을 표현하는 전치사

전치사 at, on, in은 시간을 표현할 수 있다. 한국말에서는 분, 시, 날짜, 달, 연도 등에 모두 "-에"를 붙이지만 영어에서는 이들을 구별하여 표현한다. at는 분, 시와 함께, on은 날짜와 함께, in은 달, 년, 계절과 함께 쓰인다. 그러나 몇 가지 예외가 있으니 그 표현들은 정확히 익혀 두어야 한다.

The plane will arrive **at 5 p.m.**
Wilma died **on April 6.**
Wilma moved back to Oklahoma **in 1997.**

AT with hour/minutes	ON with days / dates	IN with months/years/ seasons
at 8:00	**on** Friday	**in** May
at 3 o'clock	**on** Sundays	**in** 1988
at sunrise	**on** July 4	**in** (the) summer
at noon	**on** the weekend	**in** the morning
at midnight	**on** New Year's Day	**in** the 1990s

A. 빈칸에 알맞은 전치사를 넣어 문장을 완성하시오.

1. The movie starts (　　) 10:30.
2. I'm going to Japan (　　) July.
3. (　　) New Year's Day, I have dinner with my family.
4. I'm very busy (　　) the morning.

B. 다음 글을 읽고 틀린 부분을 찾아 맞게 고치시오.

Wilma Mankiller, the first female chief of the Cherokee Nation, passed away in April 6, 2010. She became principal chief on 1987 and led the Cherokee Nation for 10 years. At Tuesday, President Obama expressed his sadness about her death. Funeral Services will be held at the Indian Ministry, 3045 Park Avenue South, Minneapolis, at 10:00 a.m. in Wednesday, April 14.

LET'S TALK ABOUT IT

A. 다음 대화를 듣고 연습해 봅시다.

Minho: **What do you usually do in your free time?**
Chris: I usually watch movies.
Minho: Really? **Is there a movie you can recommend?**
Chris: Well... **Have you seen Mr. Bean?**
Minho: I've heard of it but I haven't seen it yet. Is it funny?
Chris: Sure. It's so funny that I laughed my head off.
Minho: Really?
Chris: You should watch it. **I guarantee** it will make you laugh.
Minho: OK. **I'll give it a try.**

B. 유용한 표현들: 소원, 기원하기

1. '한가할 때 뭐하니?'라는 표현은 **What do you usually do in your free time?** 이다.여기서 free time은 말 그대로 자유시간을 뜻한다.
2. '~추천할 것 있어'라는 표현은 **Is there ~ you can recommend?**이다. 빈칸에 a book, a place, a restaurant등을 바꿔 넣으면 된다. 그리고 다음과 같이 다르게 표현 할 수도 있다.
   - If there's an interesting movie you can recommend, please tell me. (추천할 만한 재미있는 영화 있으면 말해줘)
3. **Have you seen Mr. Bean?**는 현재 완료형을 써서 과거의 경험, 즉 미스터 빈이라는 프로를 본 적이 있냐는 뜻이다. **Have you read~?**(~을 읽어 본 적이 있니?), **Have you met~?**(~를 만난 적이 있니?)등을 함께 익혀 두면 대화에 도움이 된다.
4. **I guarantee~**(~을 보장한다)라는 뜻이고 추천 받은 일을 한 번 해 보겠다 할 때는 **I'll give it a try**라고 말하면 된다.

C. 말해보기: 아래 빈칸에 알맞은 표현을 넣으시오.

1. A: Is there a book ____________________? (추천할 만한 책 있니?)
   B: Well, how about Harry Potter? (음, 해리포터가 어때)

2. A: ________________ Harry Potter?. (해리포터 읽어 봤어)
   B: ________________ but I haven't read it yet. (들어는 봤는데 아직 안 읽어봤어.)

COMMON ERRORS IN ENGLISH

Keep health vs. Stay healthy

Sujin: You didn't come to work, Chris. What's wrong?
Chris: I had a bad cold, but I feel OK now.
Sujin: Oh, don't overwork yourself. It is important to **keep health**, Chris.
Chris: You're right. It is important to **stay healthy**.

1. '건강을 지키다' 혹은 '건강을 유지하다'라는 표현을 할 때 keep health라고 말하는 경우가 많은 데 이는 한국말을 그대로 영어로 옮긴 것으로 영어에서는 이렇게 말하지 않는다. 대신에 '~한 상태를 유지한다'라는 뜻의 stay를 사용하여 **stay healthy**라고 표현한다.

   - You should exercise regularly to **stay healthy**.
     (건강을 유지하기 위해 규칙적으로 운동해야 한다)
     그리고 그냥 '건강하다' 말할 때는 be 동사와 함께 쓴다.
   - My husband stopped smoking to **be healthy**. (내 남편은 건강을 위해 담배를 끊었다)
     그리고 Stay는 다음과 같이 사용되기도 한다.
   - **Stay safe** when you're away from home.(집을 떠나서는 안전 유의해)

2. 굳이 '건강을 유지하다"라는 표현을 하고 싶다면 maintain(유지하다)을 써서 maintain your health라고 할 수도 있다.

   - You should always try to **maintain your health**. (건강을 유지하기 위해 늘 노력해야 한다)

3. '**Don't overwork yourself**'는 너무 무리해서 일을 많이 하지 말라는 뜻이다.

Lesson 6
VOICES OF HYCU STUDENTS

Unit II People

CONTENTS

WARM UP

A. 아래 그림을 보고 질문에 답하시오

1. When was Hanyang Cyber University established?
2. How many departments are there at HYCU?
3. When was the new campus building built?

B. 대화를 듣고 질문에 답하시오

Chris: Hey, Sujin. What are you doing here?
Sujin: Hi, Chris. I'm studying for my mid- term exam.
Chris: Oh, are you getting another degree?
Sujin: Yeah, I'm studying for my BA in English at Hanyang Cyber University.
Chris: Cyber University? What is it like studying like that?
Sujin: It's great. I can study anytime and anywhere, and that's perfect for busy people like me.

1. Sujin is studying for her final exam. T F
2. Sujin majors in English. T F
3. Sujin think HYCU is perfect for busy people. T F

vocabulary

mid-term exam (중간고사 (기말 고사는 final exam))
degree (학위: (another degree 또 하나의 학위))
BA (학사학위: Bachelor's degree의 준말, MA(석사학위), Ph.D(박사학위))
What is it like studying like that? (그런 식으로 공부하는 것 어떠니?),
anytime and anywhere (언제 어디서나) major in ~ (~을 전공한다.)

VOCABULARY PREVIEW

A. 단어의 뜻과 표현을 공부해 보시오.

1. earn (벌다) to receive money in return for work
How much do you earn a month? (한달 수입은 얼마나 되십니까?)

2. wonder (궁금해하다) to want to know more about it
I wonder why she is late. (나는 왜 그녀가 늦는지 궁금하다.)

3. determined (단단히 결심한) to keep something the same
We should preserve our culture. (우리 문화를 보존해야 한다)

4. communicate (의사소통하다) to exchange information
They communicate with each other by mail. (그들은 서로 편지로 소통한다.)

5. leave (떠나다) to go away from that place or person
If you don't like it, leave! (싫으면 나가!)

6. transfer (옮겨가다) to go from one place to another
You should transfer from bus to subway. (버스에서 지하철로 갈아타야 한다.)

7. motivate (동기 부여하다) to make someone work hard
She motivated them to study hard. (그녀는 그들이 열심히 공부하게 동기를 부여했다.)

8. ideal (이상적인) perfect, or the best possible
Today is ideal for a picnic. (오늘은 소풍 가기 이상적 날이다.)

9. decision (결정) the act of making up one's mind
I will put my decision in action soon. (나는 곧 내 결심을 행동으로 하겠다.)

10. frustrating (좌절감을 갖게 하는) disappointing
It was a frustrating experience. (그건 좌절감을 느끼게 하는 경험이었다.)

B. 빈칸에 알맞은 표현을 넣으시오.

am busy (v-ing),	turn on,	succeeded in,	in the end,	look up
(-하느라 바쁘다)	(켜다)	(-에 성공하다)	(결국)	((사전등에서)-을 찾다)

1. I always (   ) new words in the dictionary.
2. I (   ) my laptop to study English.
3. People around me think I have (   ) life.
4. (   ), I was able to finish my Bachelor's degree in 3 and half years.
5. I (   ) taking challenging graduate courses.

LET'S READ IT TOGETHER

Voices of HYCU Students

1 My life is terribly busy. I am a 35-year-old mother, wife, full-time English teacher, and student at HYCU. People often call me a supermom and I'm beginning to think that I really am! I come back home from work around 7 p.m. and then do housework. Afterwards, I turn on my laptop to study with my little baby girl, Yeryn, on my lap. I usually stay up past midnight. My husband wonders why I'm so interested in my studies. I have a good reason for that: I want to go to graduate school. My life is challenging but I am determined. When my daughter brings me bread and says "Mom, eat this and then study hard!", her encouragement always helps me to keep going. (Lee, Kyung-eun)

2 People around me think I have succeeded in life. Maybe that's true because I am the owner of a manufacturing company. Over the last 30 years, I have accomplished a lot of my goals. One of my greatest achievements is entering HYCU at the age of 51 to study English. At HYCU, I had the chance to enjoy various kinds of experiences that only a student can appreciate. I participated in most extra-curricular school activities, made a lot of younger friends, won the first place prize in the English Speech Contest, and of course studied very hard. In the end, I was able to finish my Bachelor's degree in 3 and half years and entered a graduate school as Psychology major. Now, I'm busy taking challenging graduate courses. Meanwhile, I have a new plan to continue studying for my doctoral degree. Who knows, maybe I'll even become a future professor at HYCU! (Kim, Sey-yong)

Quick Comprehension Questions

1. What does Kyung-eun do first when she come back home from work?
2. How long did it take Sey-yong to graduate from HYCU?

vocabulary

terribly(대단히) housework(가사일) midnight(자정) graduate school(대학원)
encouragement(격려) manufacturing(제조업의)
extra-curricular(과외 활동) meanwhile(그동안)

3 My life has always been full of challenges. Before entering HYCU, I worked for the Korean Air Force as an air traffic controller, which I started after finishing my second year at an off-line university. My job was to communicate with pilots in English for their safety and to help guide air traffic, but I always felt that my English was lacking. One day, I happened to learn that I could earn a Bachelor's degree at a cyber university while working for the Korean Air Force. After long thought, I decided to leave my university and transfer to HYCU. It was a good decision. Everything I learned at HYCU helped me improve my English, and motivated me to go further. In a few months, I'm going to the U.S. for more language training. After that, I imagine myself working at an international airport. (Jung, Ji-hyung)

4 People often ask me why I'm studying English at my age. It wasn't an easy decision to start something new at the age of 50 after being a piano instructor for 10 years. But I've always wanted to write a novel in English, and I thought HYCU would be the ideal place for me to improve my English. For me, it is particularly hard to remember words I learn, so I always have to look up words in the dictionary. It takes a long time and sometimes, it can be frustrating. But I enjoy every minute of studying English because I can see that my English is getting better. Working toward achieving my dreams at HYCU keeps me young and energetic! (Yoon, Yang-gyun)

Quick Comprehension Questions

1. What does an air traffic controller do?
2. Why does Yang-gyun enjoy studying at HYCU?

vocabulary

air traffic controller(관제사) lacking(부족한) After long thought(오랜 생각 끝에)
particularly(특히) painful(고통스러운) toward(~을 향하여)
novel(소설) energetic(활기 찬)

READING COMPREHENSION

A. Understanding the Main Idea: 본문의 요지로 알맞은 것을 고르시오.

1. Rewarding experiences at HYCU
2. Difficulties in studying at HYCU
3. Benefits of studying at HYCU
4. Busy school life at HYCU

B. Text Organization

각각의 인물에 해당하는 내용을 찾아 쓰시오.

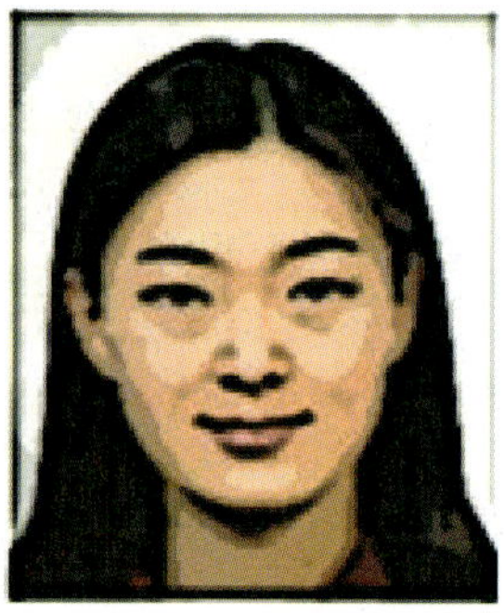			
Lee, Kyung-eun (,)	Kim, Sey-yong (,)	Jung, Ji-hyung (,)	Yoon,Yang-gyun (,)

JOBS	PLANS
a. I own a manufacturing company. b. I was an air traffic controller for the Korean Air Force. c. I am teaching English at a private language institute during the day time. d. I taught piano for more than 10 years.	1. I'm determined to go to graduate school. 2. I study English because I want to write novels in English. 3. I have a plan to continue studying for my doctoral degree. 4. I hope to work at an international airport in the future.

C. Understanding Details:
아래의 문장이 본문의 내용과 맞으면 T, 틀리면 F를 선택하시오.

	True	False
1. Kyung-eun's husband is a graduate student.		
2. Entering HYCU is one of Sye-yong's greatest achievements.		
3. Sye-yong thinks graduate courses are difficult.		
4. Ji-hyung transferred to HYCU right after he heard about cyber university.		
5. Ji-hyung is now taking language training in the U.S.		
6. Yang-gyun wrote several novels in English.		

D. Reading Strategy

글의 분위기 파악하기 (Understanding Mood)

글을 읽을 때 글쓴이의 감정과 태도 및 전체의 분위기를 파악하는 것이 글의 이해에 도움이 된다. 이것은 주로 형용사나 부사를 통해 드러난다. 명시적인 표현이 없을 때는 인물의 행동, 인물이 처한 상황 등 여러 단서를 통해 글의 분위기나 인물의 감정을 파악할 수 있다.

분위기를 표현하는 단어: **optimistic (낙관적인), pessimistic(비관적인), nervous(긴장한), boring(지루한)**

다음 글을 읽고 글의 전체적인 분위기를 적절히 나타내는 단어를 찾으시오.

For me, it is particularly hard to remember words I learned, so I always have to look up words in the dictionary. It takes a long time and sometimes, it is so frustrating. I don't think my English will get better. I want to quit school.

1. optimistic 2. pessimistic 3.sad 4. boring

Last year, my team took part in the competition. We did our best, but we did not win any awards. It was not disappointing because we learned about what our strengths and weaknesses were. Despite our high level programming skills, our English was not good enough to explain our ideas clearly to the people there. I realized that I definitely needed to improve my communication skills in English to make my dream come true.

1. optimistic 2. pessimistic 3.nervous 4. boring

VOCABULARY REVIEW

A. 빈칸에 알맞은 단어를 넣으시오.

ideal	wonder	earn	leave	motivate	determined	communicate	frustrating

1. Good teachers have to be able to (   ) their students.
2. No one knows why she had to (   ) home so suddenly.
3. I (   ) why she didn't come to class yesterday.
4. Jason failed the driving test again. It was (   ).
5. Sometimes, people (   ) with their eyes, not with words.
6. This book is easy to understand, so it is (   ) for beginners.
7. My son studies very hard to (   ) his Bachelor's degree
8. Jason lost the match last time, so he was (   ) to win this time.

B. Word Power

동사+ –ment=명사

영어에서는 동사는 뒤에 접미사를 붙여 명사로 만들 수 있는 경우가 있다.
–ment도 대단히 많이 사용되는 접미사이다.

encourage (격려하다) + ment ⇨ encouragement (격려)
achieve (성취하다) + ment ⇨ achievement (성취)
improve(개선시키다) + ment ⇨ improvement (개선)
advertise(선전하다) + ment ⇨ advertisement(선전)

1. She needed **encouragement** to continue studying.
(그녀는 학업을 계속하기 위해 격려가 필요하다)
2. When we finished the final exam, we felt a sense of **achievement**.
(기말시험을 마쳤을 때 우리는 성취감을 느꼈다)
3. Your English is much better, but there's still room for **improvement**.
(영어가 훨씬 나아졌지만 아직 개선할 여지가 있다)
4. The newspaper is full of **advertisements** for language training.
(그 신문은 언어 훈련에 대한 선전으로 차 있다)

GRAMMAR FOCUS

Frequency Adverbs (빈도 부사)

빈도 부사란 어떤 행위의 빈도를 나타내는 말이다
always ⇨ usually ⇨ often ⇨ sometimes ⇨ seldom ⇨ never
(항상) (보통) (자주) (가끔) (거의 전혀) (전혀)
문장에서 사용할 때 순서에 주의해야 한다. 즉 일반 동사의 앞에, be 동사와 조동사의 뒤에 온다.

I **always** look up words in the dictionary.
My daughter **often** brings me some bread.
My daughter brings **often** me some bread. (X)
He **seldom** smiles.

일반동사 앞, 조동사 뒤				
		빈도 부사	일반동사	
I		**always**	get up	at 6.
Jason	can	**usually**	play	tennis on Sundays.
	has	**sometimes**	cooked	Dinner for his wife.
Be 동사 뒤				
	Be	빈도 부사		
I	am	**often**		late.
Sujin	Is	**never**		late.

Be careful: often, usually, sometimes 는 문장 맨 앞이나 맨 뒤에 올 수도 있다.
Sometimes I go swimming. **Usually** I go to work on time.
Often I surf the internet. I surf the internet **often**.

A. 아래의 문장들에서 문법적으로 잘못된 부분을 찾아 올바르게 고쳐 쓰시오.

1. My father plays usually golf on Sunday.
2. I go swimming at night never.
3. I always am hungry in the afternoon.
4. Mike sometimes couldn't finish the homework on time.

B. 다음 글을 읽고 틀린 부분을 찾아 맞게 고치시오.

Kyung-eun is very busy always. She gets up usually at 6 in the morning. During the daytime, she teaches English at a private language institute. At night, she takes online lectures. She feels sometimes very tired, but she goes never to bed before midnight.

LET'S TALK ABOUT IT

A. 다음 대화를 듣고 연습해 봅시다

Karen: Wow! **The semester is almost over.**
Minho: Yeah, **time passed by so fast.** I can't believe it.
Karen: So, **what are you going to do** during the vacation?
Minho: Well, I'm going to travel.
Karen: **Have you decided where to go?**
Minho: **Not, yet,** but I want to travel abroad. How about you, Karen?
Karen: **I'm planning to** take summer session courses.
Minho: Sounds great. **I hope your plans work out.**

B. 의사소통 기능:

1. 상대방에게 무엇을 결정했는가를 묻는 표현은 **Have you decided~?**를 쓴다.
무엇을 할 지는: **what to do**, 무엇을 살 지: **what to buy**
어디에 묵을 지: **where to stay**, 어디서 살 지: **where to buy**
그리고 아직 결정하지 못했을 때는 **Not, yet**이라고 하면 된다.

2. 시간에 대한 표현으로는 **The semester is almost over.**(학기가 끝났다)에서 over는 끝났다는 표현이다. 수업이 끝났다고 하면: **School is over.**
Time passed by so fast. 시간이 참 빨리 지나갔다는 뜻이다.

3. **Summer session courses**는 여름학기 수업들을 의미한다. 그리고 '계획이 잘 진행되길 바래'라는 말은 **I hope your plans work out.**이다.

C. 말해보기: 아래 빈칸에 알맞은 표현을 넣으시오.

1. A: Have ________________ after graduation? (졸업 후 뭘 할지 결정했어?)
B: Not, yet, but I want to go to graduate school.
(아직 결정 못했지만 대학원에 가고 싶어)

2. A: I'm planning to take summer session courses. (여름학기를 들을 예정이야)
B: Sounds great. I hope ________________. (계획이 잘 진행되길 바래)

COMMON ERRORS IN ENGLISH

My English is short. vs. my English is poor.

Chris: My sister is coming to Korea next week. Can you be her tour guide?
Minho: 'Tour guide'? You know my **English is very short.**
Chris: What do you mean? Your English is short?
Minho: Ur··· I mean.. **I don't speak English very well.**
Chris: That's Ok. She can speak Korean although **her Korean is a little poor.**

1. 'My English is short"란 말은 우리가 무언가에 지식이 없거나 충분하지 않을 때 흔히 '지식이 짧다'라고 말하기 것을 그대로 영어로 옮긴 것이다. '영어를 잘 못한다'는 표현은 '**My English is poor**' 이다. 다음과 같이 표현할 수도 있다.

- My English is not very good.
- I don't speak English very well.
- My English is lacking (in vocabulary). (난 영어 단어가 부족해)

2. 참고로 '–을 잘한다'란 표현은 '**be good at**'이고 '–을 못한다'는 표현은 '**be poor at**'이다. 따라서 여기서 poor는 '가난하다'는 뜻이 아니라 '못한다'란 뜻이 된다.

- I'**m good at** mathematics. (난 수학을 잘한다)
- I'**m poor at** tennis. (난 테니스를 잘 못한다)

3. 물론 영어에서 short에는 '부족한, 열등한'이라는 뜻이 있다. 예를 들어 돈이나 시간이 부족하면 '**I'm short of money**', '**Time is short**'이고 '머리가 나쁘다'는 표현은 다음과 같다.

- He's nice, but a little **short on brains**. (그는 착하긴 한데 머리가 좀 안 좋아)

Lesson 7
WHY IS ENGLISH HARD TO LEARN?

CONTENTS

I. 영어는 왜 어려운가?

II. 영어의 어려움을 토로한 시

III. 단어의 다양한 의미

IV. 효과적인 영어학습

I. 영어는 왜 어려운가?

영어는 어렵다고 한다. 영어를 어렵게 여기는 데에는 우리말과 어순이 다르고, 단어도 다르고, 전혀 다른 문화와 사회상이 반영되었기 때문이라는 등 여러 가지가 이유가 있겠지만, 그 중 가장 흔히 거론되는 것은 영어의 불규칙성이다. 사실 영어는 다른 언어와 마찬가지로 일정한 규칙(예를 들어, 문법)을 따르고 있지만, 이와 동시에 발음, 철자, 문법(명사의 복수형, 동사의 과거형 및 분사) 등에서 너무나 많은 예외들과 예측을 어렵게 하는 불규칙성이 있기 때문에 학습자들을 이를 제대로 익히기 위해 많은 시간과 노력을 투자하면서도 늘 뭔가 부족함을 느끼곤 한다. 다음은 영어 예측 불가능성을 잘 보여주는 예들이다.

- There is no egg in **eggplant**, nor ham in **hamburger**; neither apple nor pine in **pineapple**.
  (에그플란트(가지)에는 에그가 없고 햄버거에는 햄이 없다. 파인애플에는 애플도 파인도 없다.)

- **English muffins** weren't invented in England nor **French fries** in France.
  (잉글리시 머핀은 영국에서 만들어지지 않았고, 프렌치 파이는 프랑스에서 만들어지지 않았다)

- **Sweetmeats** are candies while **sweetbreads**, which aren't sweet, are meat.
  (스윗미트(달콤한 고기)는 사탕이고 달콤한 빵(송아지의 췌장)은 달지않는 고기다.)

II. 영어는 원어민에게도 어려운 언어다

이러한 불규칙성으로 인해 영어는 단지 외국인들뿐만 아니라 영어를 모국어로 하는 사람들조차 영어를 어려워한다. 영어의 불규칙성을 생생히 드러내 보이는 다음 한 편의 시를 보면 영어란 원어민에게도 결코 만만한 언어가 아님을 알 수 있다.

English Lesson

by Richard Krogh

We'll begin with box, and the plural is boxes;
But the plural of ox should be oxen, not oxes.

Then one fowl is goose, but two are called geese
Yet the plural of moose should never be meese.

You may find a lone mouse or a whole lot of mice,
But the plural of house is houses, not hice.

If the plural of man is always called men,
When couldn't the plural of pan be called pen?

The cow in the plural may be cows or kine,
But the plural of vow is vows, not vine.

And I speak of a foot, and you show me your feet,
But I give a boot – would a pair be called beet?

If one is a tooth and a whole set are teeth,
Why shouldn't the plural of booth be called beeth?

If the singular is this and plural is these,
Why shouldn't the plural of kiss be nicknamed kese?

Then one may be that, and three may be those,
Yet the plural of hat would never be hose;

We speak of a brother, and also of brethren,
But though we say mother, we never say methren.

The masculine pronouns are he, his and him,
But imagine the feminine she, shis, and shim!

So our English, I think you will all agree,
Is the trickiest language you ever did see.

I take it you already know
Of tough and bough and cough and dough?

Others may stumble, but not you
On hiccough, thorough, slough, and through?

Well done! And now you wish, perhaps
To learn of less familiar traps?

Beware of heard, a dreadful word
That looks like beard and sounds like bird.

And dead; it's said like bed, not bead;
For goodness sake, don't call it deed!

Watch out for meat and great and threat,
(they rhyme with suite and straight and debt)

A moth is not a moth in mother.
Nor both in bother, broth in brother.

And here is not a match for there.
And dear and fear for bear and pear.

And then there's dose and rose and lose --
Just look them up -- and goose and choose.

And cork and work and card and ward,
And font and front and word and sword.

And do and go, then thwart and cart.
Come, come, I've hardly made a start.

A dreadful language? Why, man alive,
I'd learned to talk it when I was five,

And yet to write it, the more I tried,
I hadn't learned it at fifty-five!

III. 단어의 다양한 의미

그리고 영어는 방대한 양의 단어로 악명이 높다. 표현력을 기르기 위해서는 단어를 많이 알고 있어야 하는 것이 기본인데, 영어 단어는 누구도 정확한 숫자를 알 수 없을 정도로 많고 과학 기술의 발전과 사회 변화로 인해 매년 그 수가 증가하고 있다. 더구나 우리가 알고 있는 단어 조차도 형태가 똑같음에도 불구하고 다른 품사로 사용되거나 뜻이 전혀 다르게 사용되는 경우가 많아 늘 우리를 당혹스럽게 만든다. 다음의 예들을 보자.

- I saw a lot of **fish** around here, so I'll stay and **fish** some more.

이 문장에서 첫 번째 fish는 명사로 "물고기"라는 뜻이고 두 번째는 "낚시하다"는 동사로 쓰였다. 그래도 이 문장에서 fish는 의미상으로는 서로 연관이 있지만, 다음 문장들의 경우에는 상황이 전혀 다르다.

- The Internet has **change**d the way people work.
- You can keep the **change**.

앞의 문장에서는 change가 동사로 "변화시키다"라는 뜻으로 쓰였지만, 뒷 문장에서는 "잔돈, 거스름돈"이라는 뜻으로 쓰였다. 물론 곰곰히 생각하면 지폐를 주고 변한 것(남은 것)이니 잔돈일 것이라 추측이 가능하지만, change를 변화(하다)로만 알고 있을 경우 두 번째 문장을 들었을 때 바로 뜻을 알아차리지 못할 가능성이 높다. 이렇듯 영어 단어는 뜻이 고정되어 있지 않고 품사도 고정되어 있지 않은 경우가 많다. 뜻과 품사는 문장 안에서 어떻게 사용되는가에 따라 결정된다. 즉 단어가 사용되는 맥락(context)이 중요하다.

IV. 효과적인 영어학습

그렇다면 영어 공부는 어떻게 해야 효과적일까? 영어의 중요성이 높아지면서 인터넷 등지에 너무나 많은 조언들이 난무하고 있다. 대부분이 나름 일리가 있는 내용들이라 여기서는 그런 조언들이 놓치고 있는 부분만 간략히 제시한다.

1. 영어 공부는 반드시 본인이 직접 소리를 내며 해야 한다. 영어는 언어, 즉 소리를 기반으로 한 의사소통의 형태이기 때문이다.
2. 한국어의 도움을 받되 이를 최소한으로 해야 한다. 정 영어가 어려워 한국말로 해석을 해서 이해를 하더라도 거기서 멈추지 말고 반드시 마지막에 영어로 읽으며 (또는 말하며) 그대로 이해하려고 노력해야 한다.
3. 한국어로 정확히 1대1로 번역하려는 시도, 혹은 그 반대루 한국어를 영어로 정확히 번역하려는 시도는 자제해야 한다. 두 언어 사이에는 차이가 크기 때문에 애당초 정확한 1대1 관계는 성립하지 않는다.
4. 영어 단어 뜻이나 품사가 고정되어 있다는 생각을 버려야 한다. 아래 예문에서는 kind가 모양이 같아도 품사와 뜻이 다르게 쓰였지만 여러분 대부분은 kind의 뜻을 정확히 이해 할 수 있을 것이다.

- There are many **kind**s of flowers in the garden.
- He is a very **kind** man.

이는 여러분이 kind의 뜻을 하나로 고정해서 알고 있지 않기 때문이다.

5. 뜻에 확신이 서지 않는 단어는 반드시 사전을 찾아 보고 정리해야 한다. 그리고 공부한 내용을 노트에 기록해 수시로 틈틈이 연습해 보아야 한다.
6. 가장 결정적으로는 새로 배우게 된(알게 된) 표현을 실제 상황에서 써 보아야 한다. 해도 잊어 버린다는 말을 많이 하는 데 이는 충분히 하지 않았기 때문이고, 막연히 기계적으로 외웠기 때문이다. 암기는 중요하지만 자기 자신에게 의미있는 방식으로 연습하지 않으면 잊어 버리는 것은 당연한 것이다.
7. 좀 못하는 느낌이 들어도 절대 기 죽으면 안 된다. 원어민에게도 영어는 어렵다. 기본적인 의사 소통 능력을 제대로 습득하는 데에도 수 년이 걸린다. 현재의 실력에 실망하지 말고, 지금 현재 배우고 있는 내용을 충실히 꾸준히 하면 누구나 할 수 있다. 언어는 인간의 기본 능력이고 누구나 이 능력을 가지고 있기 때문이다.

"I hear and I forget. I see and I remember. I do and I understand."
(나는 듣고, 잊어 버린다. 보고, 기억한다. 하고, 이해한다)

Unit II People

Lesson 8
WRITING TIPS

CONTENTS

Punctuation: 대문자 사용법

Punctuation: 콤마 (나열항목에서의 용법)

Punctuation: 콤마 (문장을 시작하는 구와 절에서의 용법)

I. Capitalization

A. Rules

Rule 1. The first letter of a sentence

Ex) every year, many people visit the Arboretum.(X)
Every year, many people visit the Arboretum.(O)

Rule 2. The pronoun I:

Ex) My friend and i went to Chollipo. (X)
My friend and I went to Chollipo. (O)

Rule 3. Proper nouns: specific and unique people, places, or things.

Ex) a. a person's name: bill clinton (X) Bill Clinton (O)
b. a place name: africa (X) Africa (O)
c. months, days of the week: june (X) June (O)
d. monday (X) Monday (O)

B. 아래의 문장에서 대문자로 써야 하는 철자에 동그라미를 하시오.

1. My birthday is next friday.
2. Her favorite actor is tom cruise.
3. Some people don't know korea is located in asia.
4. americans celebrate martin luther king day in the winter.

C. 다음 글을 읽고 틀린 부분을 찾아 고치시오

my name is carl Miller. i was born in pennsylvania, u.s.a. in 1921. i served the u.s. navy during world war II and then came to korea in 1945. From early 1970s, i started to build a garden in chollipo and I finally established the chollipo arboretum. it was awarded the "Arboretum Distinguished for Merit", the first time in asia.

II. Comma (,) with Items in a Series

A. Rules

Rule 1. Use a comma to separate three or more items in a series.

Ex) They are found in foods such as rice, breads, and potatoes. (O)
They are found in foods such as rice breads and potatoes. (X)

Rule 2. Do not use a comma if there are only two items.

Ex) Limit sugar and salt. (O)
Limit sugar, and salt. (X)

B. 아래 문장에서 필요한 곳에 콤마를 넣으시오. (콤마가 필요 없는 문장도 있습니다.)

1. Fish poultry and eggs are important sources of protein.
2. It should contain essential nutrients such as carbohydrates fats protein minerals and vitamins.
3. My sister always eats fruits and vegetables for lunch.
4. Karen Andy and Paul like to eat Ramen.
5. Nuts and seeds are good sources of healthy fats.

C. 다음 글을 읽고 틀린 부분을 찾아 맞게 고치시오.

My brother and I have different tastes of foods. For example, I like to have eggs bacon and coffee for breakfast. But my brother eats toast fruits and milk in the morning. So my mother is very busy preparing them every morning. Usually Mom goes grocery shopping to buy milk orange juice coffee bacon and eggs. But I changed my mind to eat different kinds of food. Yesterday, I went grocery shopping. I bought bread cereal apples bananas and tomatoes. My brother was very glad because he could eat apples and bananas.

III. Comma (,) with Introductory Phrases and Clauses

A. 문장을 시작하는 구나 절 뒤에 콤마를 찍는다.

Rule 1. Use a comma after an introductory phrase (a word or word group) to help readers sort sentence parts.

Ex) Similarly, some people say that we might have a critical period in learning our language. (O)
Similarly some people say that we might have a critical period in learning our language. (X)

Rule 2. Use a comma after an introductory clause to help readers distinguish it from the main clause.

Ex) If some birds miss these certain periods, they may never learn to sing. (O)
If some birds miss these certain periods they may never learn to sing. (X)

B. 아래 문장에서 필요한 곳에 콤마를 넣으시오.

1. Before Victor was found he apparently lived his entire childhood alone in the woods.
2. Occasionally Victor spoke a few words, but that was all.
3. For one thing Korean parents seem to wish that at least their children's pronunciation will be very good.
4. According to some studies motivation, anxiety, and time commitment are equally important.
5. When I entered the first grade in elementary school I began learning how to read.

C. 다음 글을 읽고 틀린 부분을 찾아 맞게 고치시오.

Around the time I reached puberty, I began learning English. When I was a student in elementary school English was not an official subject to study. At the age of 14 I started learning the English alphabet. Because I wanted to understand what American people said on TV I studied English very hard. I also enjoyed learning English and spent a lot of time in speaking and listening to English. Finally when I was a senior at university, I was chosen to study abroad in the U.S.

Lesson 9

LANGUAGE LEARNING FACTORS

CONTENTS

Reading: 언어습득의 중요한 요인들

Reading Strategy: 주제문과 뒷받침 문장 구별하기

Word Power: 명사 + -ful

Grammar Focus: 수동태

Let's Talk About It: (다시 만날 것을) 제안 및 식사 대접하기

Common Errors in English: Elder vs. Older

WARM UP

A. 아래 그림을 보고 질문에 답하시오.

1. Who are in these pictures?
2. What are they doing?
3. Can we learn a foreign language as adults?

B. 대화를 듣고 T 또는 F를 고르시오.

Sujin: Look who's here!
Chris: Oh, Hi, Sujin! What are you doing here?
Sujin: I'm waiting for my son. He'll arrive soon from LA.
Chris: From LA? Is he studying in the States?
Sujin: Yeah, but he's coming back to spend his vacation with my family.
Chris: Oh, I see. He's my daughter's age, so he's 12 this year, right?
Sujin: That's right.

1. Chris and Sujin know each other.	T	F
2. Sujin's son is studying at a US college.	T	F
3. Chris has a young daughter.	T	F

vocabulary

Look who's here! (아니, 이게 누구예요?)
What are you doing here? (여기는 어쩐 일이예요?)
arrive (at).. ((..에) 도착하다: arrive to가 아니므로 주의)
the States (미국)　　spend ((시간을) 보내다)

VOCABULARY PREVIEW

A. 단어의 뜻과 표현을 공부해 보세요

1. expert (전문가) someone who is very knowledgeable about something
a bird expert (새 전문가)

2. critical (매우 중요한) very important
This contract is critical for our company's future.(이 계약은 우리 회사에게 굉장히 중요하다.)

3. early (일찍) before the usual or expected time
I arrived at the meeting early. (나는 일찍 그 회의에 도착했다.)

4. difficulty (문제, 어려움) a problem or not easily done
have difficulty understanding the question (그 질문을 이해하는데 어려움이 있다.)

5. age (나이) years a person has lived
We are the same age. (우리는 나이가 같다.)

6. acquire (습득하다) to learn or get
Is it really difficult to acquire a foreign language? (외국어를 배우는 건 정말 어려운 거니?)

7. lock (잠그다) to fasten something with a key
I accidentally locked my cat in my car. (우연히 차에 고양이를 두고 차를 잠갔다.)

8. human (인간, 사람) a person
Can humans live in Antarctica? (사람들은 남극에 살 수 있을까?)

9. possible (가능한) able to be done or likely
What are some possible causes of the disease? (그 병의 가능한 발병 원인들은 무엇인가?)

10. existence (존재, 실재) living or being real
Many people believe in the existence of aliens. (많은 사람들은 외계인이 존재한다고 믿고 있다.)

B. 빈칸에 알맞은 표현을 넣으시오.

by herself (혼자)	ended up (결국…하게 되었다)	in the first place (먼저, 우선)	go on (계속…하다)	make our best efforts (최선의 노력을 하다)

1. Of course, birds can sing, but how did they learn ( )?
2. Before Genie was found, she lived in a dark, locked room ( ).
3. As a result, Genie ( ) only learning about 100 words.
4. If we continue to ( ), we can acquire great English skills.
5. "Why do the birds ( ) singing?" This is part of the lyrics of an old American pop song, "The End of the World."

LET'S READ IT TOGETHER

Language Learning Factors

1 "Why do the birds go on singing?" This is part of the lyrics of an old American pop song, "The End of the World." Although the song is about love, it asks an interesting question: Why and how do birds sing in the first place? Experts say that some birds learn to sing from older birds early in life, so if these birds miss this chance to learn their songs, they will have great difficulty learning to sing later on. People call this time the "critical period." More importantly, some language experts argue that this critical period might also apply to humans, along with some other possible factors for learning a language.

2 One classic demonstration of the existence of the critical period can be seen with a girl named Genie. She was found in 1970 in California at the age of 13 but could not speak except for short phrases like "Stop it." Before she was found, she lived in a dark, locked room by herself. Almost no one, not even her parents, met or talked with her often. As a result, she ended up only learning about 100 words from language specialists who tried to teach her English.

bird

parent

Quick Comprehension Questions

1. What is the song, "The End of the World" about?
2. When do some birds learn to sing?

vocabulary

lyrics (가사) miss (놓치다) period (시기, 기간)
argue (주장하다) factor (요인) classic (고전적인)

3 Genie's case is about acquiring a first language, but what about learning a foreign language? Should we begin learning English early in life to be successful? Language experts generally believe that to acquire a foreign language, younger is better. More specifically, they say that to get native-like fluency, we should learn a foreign language before puberty.

4 However, research shows that there are also other important factors in learning a foreign language, such as motivation and time commitment. In other words, if a person is highly motivated to learn English and invests enough time, English skills can improve. Younger learners may be more fluent and have better pronunciation, but older learners can still learn the language and communicate without much difficulty.

5 In fact, the ability to successfully communicate is actually more important. There may be a critical period with some birds and with some people, but there is hope. If we continue to make our best efforts, we can speak better English and can be successful communicators. So, don't give up. Remember that motivation and time are also important.

Quick Comprehension Questions

1. To get native-like fluency, when might be the best time to learn a foreign language?
2. Age is an important factor for learning a language. What else is important in improving English?

vocabulary

puberty (사춘기) fluent (유창한) pronunciation (발음)
motivation (자극, 동기) commitment (투입) effort (노력)

READING COMPREHENSION

A. Understanding the Main Idea: 본문의 요지로 알맞은 것을 고르시오.

1. The lives of some special birds
2. Factors that affect language learning
3. Why birds sing and how they learn to sing
4. A case study of an American girl called Genie

B. Text Organization

다음은 본문의 각 단락의 내용을 요약한 것으로, 어느 단락의 내용인지 그 단락의 번호를 적으시오.

P ______ To explain the role of a critical period on first language acquisition

P ______ To introduce the term "critical period" for birds and its meaning for people

P ______ To show other important factors for learning a foreign language other than age

P ______ To point out that younger is better for foreign language acquisition

P ______ To conclude by stating that age is not the only factor for acquiring a foreign language and that older learners can improve their English if they do not give up

C. Understanding Details:

아래의 문장이 본문의 내용과 맞으면 T, 틀리면 F를 선택하시오.

	True	False
1. Genie grew up as an orphan.		
2. When Genie was found, she was almost 3 years old.		
3. Language specialists tried to learn from Genie a foreign language.		
4. Genie was able to form sentences in English after studying it.		
5. After puberty, a foreign language may be more difficult to acquire.		
6. Being able to communicate effectively is more important than having good pronunciation in a foreign language.		

D. Reading Strategy

주제문과 뒷받침 문장 구별하기
(Distinguishing the Topic Sentence from Supporting Details)

하나의 단락은 전체 내용을 포괄하는 주제문과 그 내용을 구체적으로 설명하는 뒷받침 문장들로 구성된다. 주제문이 너무 광범위하면 구체화 시킬 때 어렵고, 너무 구체적이면 뒷받침 문장들이 필요 없게 된다. 주제문은 보통 한 문장 또는 두 문장으로 간결히 표현되고, 뒷받침 문장들은 구체적인 사실, 예시, 이유, 설명, 묘사, 경험 등의 내용이 온다.

본문의 둘째 단락을 주제문과 뒷받침 문장으로 분석하시오. 어느 문장이 주제문이고, 어느 문장들이 뒷받침 문장들인지 각각의 문장 옆에 그 기능을 적으시오. (S1 은 첫째 문장을 의미한다.)

1. S1: ______________________ 2. S2: ______________________

3. S3: ______________________ 4. S4: ______________________

5. S5: ______________________

VOCABULARY REVIEW

A. 빈칸에 알맞은 단어를 넣으시오.

lyrics	factors	critical	age	expert	apply	dark	research

1. Go out and play but come home before it gets (   ).
2. My sister and I are the same (   ) because we are twins.
3. My brother is a computer (   ). He knows all about computers.
4. To improve your English, your willingness to communicate is (   ).
5. According to previous (   ), to live longer, we should think positively.
6. To be fair, the same rules must (   ) to everyone.
7. Poverty is one of the possible (   ) of why crime occurs.
8. A good melody is important, but I prefer songs with good (   ).

B. Word Power

명사 + –ful = 형용사

접미사 –ful을 붙이면 품사만 형용사로 변하는 명사들이 있다. 하지만 그 변화 과정에서 "자음 + y"로 끝나는 명사는 y가 i로 변하기 때문에 이와 같은 경우(예: beautiful)는 주의해야 한다.

success (성공) + ful ⇨ successful (성공적인)
care (조심) + ful ⇨ careful (조심하는)
sorrow (큰 슬픔) + ful ⇨ sorrowful (아주 슬픈)
beauty (아름다움) + ful ⇨ beautiful (아름다운)

1. The weather is **beautiful** today.
2. Whenever I hear that sad song, I'm filled with **sorrowful** memories.
3. Always be **careful** when you drive, especially when the road is wet.
4. To be **successful** at work, you should be knowledgeable about your company.

GRAMMAR FOCUS

The Passive Voice (수동태)

영어의 다양한 형식 중에는 능동태와 수동태란 것이 존재한다. 행하는 주체가 주어의 자리에 오게 되면 이는 능동태의 형식이 되고, 행함을 받게 되는 주체가 주어의 자리에 오게 되면 이는 수동태의 형식이 된다. 예를 들어,

능동태: This book changed my life. — 일반동사

수동태: My life was changed by this book. — be동사+일반동사의 과거분사

Can you read this letter? It **is written** (by S) in English.
I have a sofa in my office, and it **is used** (by S) sometimes as my bed.

규칙동사	불규칙동사
use – used – used	sell – sold – sold
hire – hired – hired	build – built – built
raise – raised – raised	write – wrote – written
discover – discovered – discovered	speak – spoke – spoken

* 부록 참고

A. 괄호 안의 어휘를 문장에 알맞은 형태로 변형하여 빈칸에 넣으시오.

1. My house (   ) in 2009. (build)
2. French (   ) in some parts of Canada. (speak)
3. My brother and I (   ) by our grandparents. (raise)
4. Many people think that America (   ) by Columbus. (discover)

B. 다음 글을 읽고 틀린 부분을 찾아 맞게 고치시오.

Genie found in 1970 in California. When she finds, she was 13 years old but could not speak except for short phrases. The reason was because she tie to a potty chair until she became 13 years old and leave alone in a dark room. Almost no one, not even her parents, met or talked with her often.

LET'S TALK ABOUT IT

A. 다음 대화를 듣고 연습해 봅시다.

Sujin: Are you waiting for someone here, too?
Chris: Yes, my wife. You've met her before, right?
Sujin: Of course! I like her a lot. She's very easy to talk to.
Chris: Thanks. She's coming back from Chicago. Her parents live there.
Sujin: I see. By the way, **we should get together again sometime**. It was fun last time!
Chris: Yeah, it was. Last time **it was our treat**, so this time **it's on you**!
Sujin: No problem! You are welcome at any time!
Chris: Thanks! Oh here she comes!

B. 유용한 표현들

1. "우리 언제 다시 한번 모여야지" 라고 제안하고 싶을 때 We should get together again sometime의 표현이 가능하다. 이 외의 다른 표현으로는 다음이 가능하다.

Let's get together again sometime. (우리 언제 다시 모이자.)
Why don't we get together again sometime? (우리 언제 다시 모이는 게 어때?)

2. "내가 살께" 라는 의미로 It's my treat 또는 It's on me의 표현이 가능하지만 음식점, 술집과 같은 곳에서 고객에게 서비스를 제공할 때는 It's on the house란 표현을 쓴다.

(At a restaurant)
Customer: I didn't order this. (이건 주문하지 않았는데요.)
Server: **It's on the house**. (서비스입니다.)
Customer: Oh. Thank you very much. (감사합니다.)

C. 말해보기: 아래 빈칸에 알맞은 표현을 넣으시오.

1. A: I had fun last month! (지난 달에 정말 재미있었는데!)
   B: Me, too! ______________________________ (나도! 우리 언제 다시 한번 모여야지.)

2. A: Since you bought dinner, ______________ (네가 저녁을 샀으니, 커피는 내가 살께!)
   B: Sounds good! (좋아!)

Elder vs. Older

Sujin: I saw your brother yesterday. He's elder than you, right?
Chris: Right, but we don't say "He's elder than you."
Sujin: How do you say it then?
Chris: We say **"He's older than you."**

1. Elder란 형용사는 older와 그 형태에 있어서 비슷해 보이지만 older보다 제한적인 용법으로 사용된다. 예를 들어, elder는 than과 함께 쓰이지 않는다. 따라서 바른 표현은 다음과 같다.

   He's elder than you, right? ⇨ He's **older than** you, right?
   (그는 너보다 나이가 많지, 그지?)

2. Elder는 형용사로 쓰일 때, 명사와 함께 사용되거나 독립적으로 사용된다. Older역시 elder대신 사용될 수 있다. 하지만 요즘 시대의 사람들이 흔히 사용하는 단어는 elder/eldest가 아니라 older/oldest이다. (Eld라는 말은 없음)

   Chris has an **elder/older brother**. (크리스는 형이 한 명 있다.)

   I have two sons, James and John. James is **the elder/older (son)**.
   (나에게는 제임스와 존이라는 두 명의 아들이 있다. 그 중 제임스가 형이다.)

   I have three children, James, John, and Ann. James is **the eldest/oldest (child)**.
   (나에게는 제임스, 존, 앤이라는 세명의 아이들이 있다. 그 중 제임스가 맏이다.)

Lesson 10

BODY LANGUAGE DIFFERS AROSS CULTURES

CONTENTS

Reading: 문화에 따라 차이가 나는 몸짓언어

Reading Strategy: 결론 이끌어 내기

Word Power: 형용사 + –ly

Grammar Focus: 최상급의 형용사

Let's Talk About It: 본인의 생각 밝히기

Common Errors in English: Fighting! vs. You can do it!

WARM UP

A. 아래 그림을 보고 질문에 답하시오.

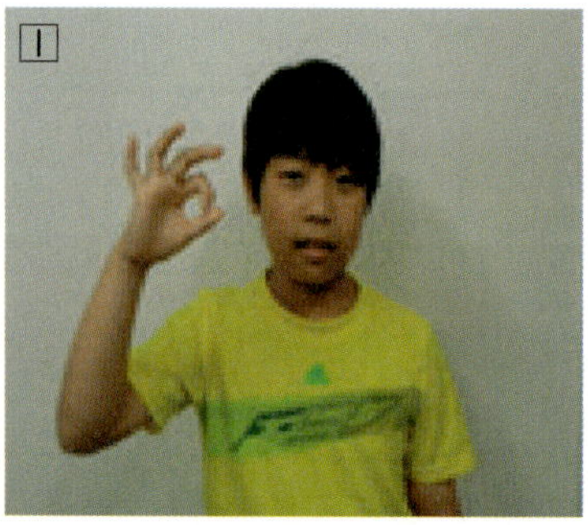

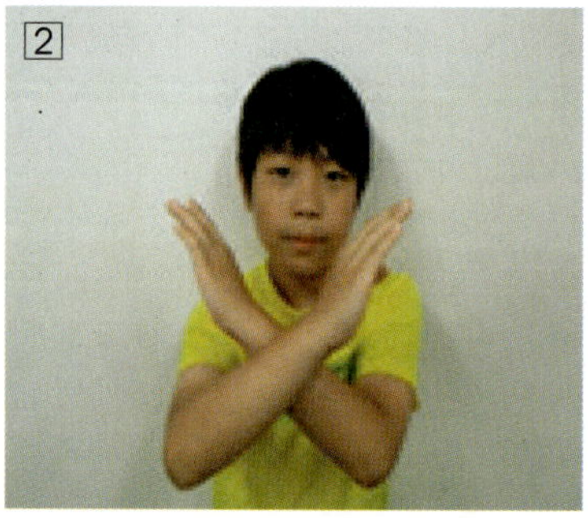

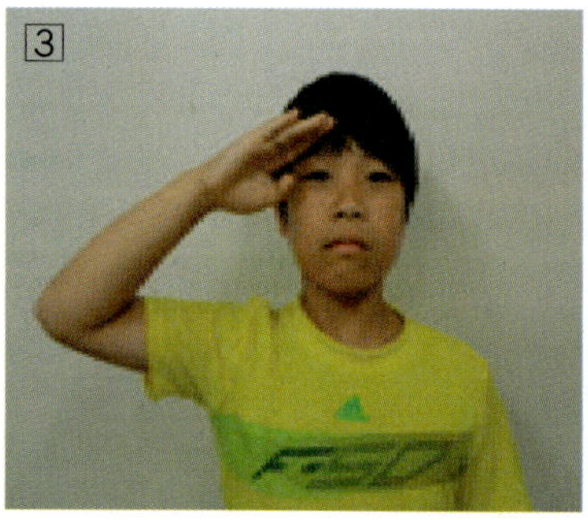

1. What might the gesture mean in picture 1?
2. What might the gesture mean in picture 2?
3. What might the gesture mean in picture 3?

B. 대화를 듣고 T 또는 F를 고르시오.

Chris: Sujin, did you know that body language can differ across cultures?
Sujin: Yeah, just like languages are different.
Chris: What gesture do you use for money in Korea?
Sujin: We make a circle using the thumb and the index finger.
Chris: I see. That's interesting. Do you know how we show money in the U.S.?
Sujin: I'm not sure, but isn't it by rubbing the thumb against the index and middle fingers?

1. Sujin understands that body language can differ across cultures. T F
2. In Korea, the gesture for money is making a circle using the thumb and finger. T F
3. Chris is showing Sujin how to indicate money with American body language. T F

vocabulary

thumb (엄지손가락) rub (문지르다) index finger (집게 손가락)
Two thumbs up! (어떤 것을 굉장히 좋아할 때 사용할 수 있는 표현)
(A: How was the food/the movie? B: Two thumbs up! = It was great!)

VOCABULARY PREVIEW

A. 단어의 뜻과 표현을 공부해 보세요.

1. convey (전달하다) to communicate a thought, feeling, or idea
convey a message (메시지를 전달하다)

2. way (방법) a method of doing something
What's the best way to learn a language? (언어를 배우는 가장 좋은 방법은 무엇인가?)

3. opposite (정반대, 정반대의) (a thing) most different from something
in the opposite direction (정반대 방향으로)

4. nod (고개를 끄덕이다) to move one's head down and then up
nod one's head (머리를 끄덕이다)

5. invade (침입, 침범하다) to enter a place by force
The ants invaded the kitchen. (그 개미들이 부엌을 침범했다.)

6. space (공간) an empty area
Can we make space for an extra desk? (책상 하나 더 놓을 공간 만들 수 있을까?)

7. rude (무례한, 예의 없는) offensively not polite
Why were you so rude to James? (제임스에게 왜 그렇게 무례하게 대했니?)

8. different (다른) not the same
I'm very different from my older sister. (나는 언니와는 매우 다르다.)

9. typical (전형적인, 대표적인) usual, common (characteristic)
a typical summer day (전형적인 여름날)

10. actually (사실은) really, in fact
Am I annoyed? No, I'm actually relieved. (내가 짜증났냐고? 아니, 사실은 마음이 놓여.)

B. 빈칸에 알맞은 표현을 넣으시오.

call over (..을 부르다)	In parts of (..의 일부 지역에서는)	go to (..로 가다)
It seems that (..인 듯 생각되다)	more than (..이상의)	

1. (　　　　　) speaking is the most important way to communicate.
2. Interestingly, however, this is how we (　　　　　) our pets!
3. (　　　　　) Greece and Turkey, they indicate "yes" by shaking their head.
4. If you (　　　　　) Spain, be aware that they don't have this notion of personal space.
5. (　　　　　) half of what we communicate is actually conveyed through body language.

LET'S READ IT TOGETHER

Body Language Differs Across Cultures

1 When we talk about "communication," the first thing that comes to mind is probably one person talking and another person listening. In other words, it seems that speaking is the most important way to communicate. However, experts say that more than half of what we communicate is actually conveyed through body language. They argue that this silent language is as important as speaking because body language has its own meanings, which can also be different across cultures.

2 Hand gestures are a typical example. In Korea, when we signal someone to "come here," we face the palm downward and move our fingers back and forth. However, the American way of showing the "come here" gesture is the exact opposite of the Korean way. Their palm is upward, and they move their fingers back and forth at the same time. This gesture can be used for children or animals. Similarly, the gesture is also used in Korea but only when we call over pets. So, if it is used for people, it can be considered very rude.

palm

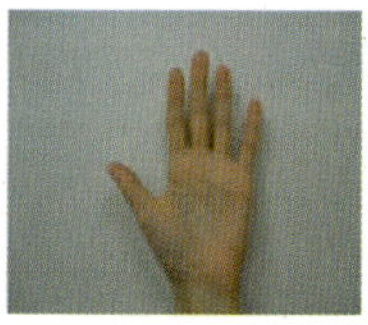

fingers

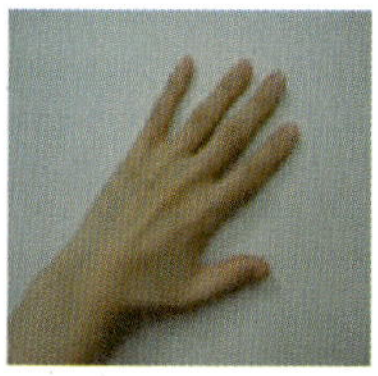

American "come here" gesture

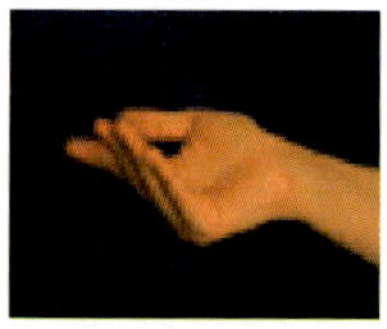

Quick Comprehension Questions

1. What is a different word for body language?
2. Are words the main means to communicate your meaning?
3. How much is understood by body language?

vocabulary

mind (머리) half (절반) face (..을 향하다) downward (아래쪽을 향하여)
mistake (오해하다) back and forth (앞뒤로) means (방법)

3 Another example is a particular head gesture. In most of the world, including Korea, people indicate "yes" by nodding their head up and down. To mean "no," they shake their head side to side. However, in some parts of the world, people use these gestures in the opposite way. In parts of Greece, Yugoslavia, Bulgaria, and Turkey, people indicate "yes" by shaking their head and "no" by nodding it. So, if you happen to travel to one of these areas, you should remember this difference.

4 Body language is not always about body parts such as the hands and the head. Personal space is also a part of body language that can have different meanings. In the U.S., for example, people do not stand too close to each other so as not to invade one another's comfort zone. However, if you go to Spain, you will find that they do not have this notion of personal space. You can see this amusing scene in Spain: in a conversation, if an American person steps backward from a Spanish person in order to feel more comfortable, the Spanish will actually step forward to reduce the distance between them!

5 In short, body language has its own meanings, just like words. The meanings are also different across cultures. So, if you are traveling abroad, be sure to study that country's body language. It can make your trip either a pleasant or a frustrating experience. Remember that sometimes "actions speak louder than words!"

personal space

travel

study

Quick Comprehension Questions

1. What is a different word for personal space?
2. What does "actions speak louder than words!" mean?

vocabulary

part (..의 일부, 부분) amusing (재미있는) backward (뒤로)
forward (앞으로) notion (개념) abroad (해외로, 해외에서)

READING COMPREHENSION

A. Understanding the Main Idea: 본문의 요지로 알맞은 것을 고르시오.

1. The importance of understanding personal space for communication
2. The importance of understanding hand gestures for communication
3. The importance of understanding head gestures for communication
4. The importance of understanding body language for communication

B. Text Organization

다음은 본문의 각 단락의 내용을 요약한 것으로, 어느 단락의 내용인지 그 단락의 번호를 적으시오.

P _____ To describe how the same head gesture can be understood differently across cultures

P _______ To describe how the same hand gestures can be understood differently between cultures

P ______ To conclude by restating the main point with some suggestion for future use

P _______ To describe how the idea of personal space can be understood differently between cultures

P _______ To introduce the topic by contrasting what we think with what experts say

C. Understanding Details:
아래의 문장이 본문의 내용과 맞으면 T, 틀리면 F를 선택하시오.

	True	False
1. The American "come here" gesture is usually used for children or animals.		
2. If the "come here" gesture for Americans is used in Korea to call people, it will be viewed as insulting.		
3. In some parts of Greece, people nod their heads to mean "come here."		
4. Body language is only about using body parts.		
5. In Spain, people tend to stand very close to each other while having a conversation.		
6. If you plan to visit a foreign country, it is a good idea to first learn about the body language there before you arrive.		

D. Reading Strategy

결론 이끌어 내기 (Drawing a Conclusion)

하나의 글은 서론 (introduction), 본론 (body), 결론 (conclusion)으로 구성될 수 있는데, 결론은 전체 글의 요지를 담고 있다. 올바른 결론을 도출하기 위해서는 본론의 내용을 이해함과 더불어 전체 글의 맥락을 이해하여야 한다. 결론에서 주로 언급되는 내용으로는 요약(summary)과 함께 본론에서 다루어졌던 내용과 관련된 추측 (prediction), 추천 (recommendation), 또는 해결방안 (solution) 등이 있다.

본문의 마지막 단락에서 아래의 문장들이 어떤 내용 (요약, 추측, 추천)을 담고 있는지 분석하시오.

1. Sentences 1+2: ______________________

2. Sentence 3: ______________________

3. Sentence 4: ______________________

VOCABULARY REVIEW

A. 빈칸에 알맞은 단어를 넣으시오.

abroad	convey	way	signal	rude	opposite	including	mistaken

1. Using gestures while speaking is a way to ( ) emphasis.
2. While driving, I sometimes forget to ( ) before I change lanes on the road.
3. What's the ( ) of the word, "forward"?
4. Is there an easy ( ) to learn a foreign language?
5. Asking a stranger personal questions can be considered ( ).
6. I will have a three-day weekend break ( ) Monday.
7. Have you ever worked ( )?
8. Because of how I look, I'm often ( ) as a foreigner.

B. Word Power

형용사 + -ly = 부사

형용사에 접미사 -ly를 붙이면 부사로 변하는 경향이 있다. 하지만 그 변화 과정에서 "자음 + y"로 끝나는 형용사는 y가 i로 변하기 때문에 이와 같은 경우(예: happily)는 주의해야 한다.

important (중요한) + ly ⇨ importantly (중요하게)
interesting (흥미로운) + ly ⇨ interestingly (흥미롭게도)
different (다른) + ly ⇨ differently (다르게)
exact (정확한) + ly ⇨ exactly (정확하게)
happy (행복한) + ly ⇨ happily (행복하게)

1. **Interestingly**, his memory improves as he gets older.
2. Jennifer acted **differently** today than she did yesterday.
3. The accident occurred **exactly** one year ago today.
4. The prince and princess lived **happily** ever after.

GRAMMAR FOCUS

Superlative Adjectives (최상급의 형용사)

최상급은 "the -est, the most ‥ " 의 형태로, "가장 -한" 의 의미를 가진다. 짧은 단어일 경우, "the -est" 를 붙이고, 긴 단어일 경우 "the most" 를 붙인다.

I believe that my mother is **the kindest** person in the world.
Body language can be **the most important** part of communication.

짧은 단어	긴 단어
kind-kinder-the kindest	different-more different-the most different
close-closer-the closest	personal-more personal-the most personal
rude-ruder-the rudest	important-more important-the most important
loud-louder-the loudest	interesting-more interesting-the most interesting

* 부록 참고

A. 괄호 안의 어휘를 최상급의 형태로 빈칸에 넣으시오.

1. Where is (   ) supermarket around here? (close)
2. My friend, Jenny, is (   ) person in the world! (loud)
3. This is (   ) book I have ever read. (interesting)
4. Asking someone about his or her salary is one of (   ) questions to ask. (personal)

B. 다음 글을 읽고 틀린 부분을 찾아 맞게 고치시오.

When we talk about cultural differences, body language is perhaps most interesting topic to discuss. One of most obvious differences can be seen in people's hand gestures. In Korea, for the "come here" gesture, the palm is downward and the fingers are moved back and forth. However, in the U.S., they show the "come here" gesture in the opposite way. Their palm is upward, and they move their fingers back and forth.

LET'S TALK ABOUT IT

A. 다음 대화를 듣고 연습해 봅시다.

Sujin: Chris, I want to ask you about something.
Chris: Sure. What is it?
Sujin: One day, I was waiting in line at the airport.
Chris: And?
Sujin: And I was talking with an American lady but I noticed her moving from me.
Chris: Were you standing too close to her?
Sujin: **I don't think** I was. But … maybe she thought I was talking too close to her?
Chris: That's possible. When I stood in line in Korea, I sometimes felt uncomfortable because people stood too close to me.

B. 유용한 표현들

1. 자신의 생각을 밝힐 때, I think란 표현도 사용할 수 있다.

I think this drawing is excellent.
I think I was standing too close to her.

2. 위의 문장들과 반대의 의미를 표현하고 싶을 때 "I think + 부정의 동사" 를 생각할 수 있지만 "I don't think + 긍정의 동사" 가 더 자연스러운 표현이다.

I think this drawing **isn't** excellent. (부자연)
I don't think this drawing **is** excellent. (자연)

I think I **wasn't** standing too close to her. (부자연)
I don't think I **was** standing too close to her. (자연)

C. 말해보기: 아래 빈칸에 알맞은 표현을 넣으시오.

1. A: What are your thoughts about the soccer match? (축구 경기 어땠다고 생각해?)
   B: We lost, but ____________ we did well. (우리가 지긴 했지만, 그래도 내 생각에는 잘한 것 같아.)

2. A: What are your thoughts about the soccer match? (축구 경기 어땠다고 생각해?)
   B: We won, but ____________ we did well. (우리가 이기긴 했는데, 내 생각에 잘 했던 건 아닌 것 같아.)

COMMON ERRORS IN ENGLISH

Fighting! vs. You can do it!

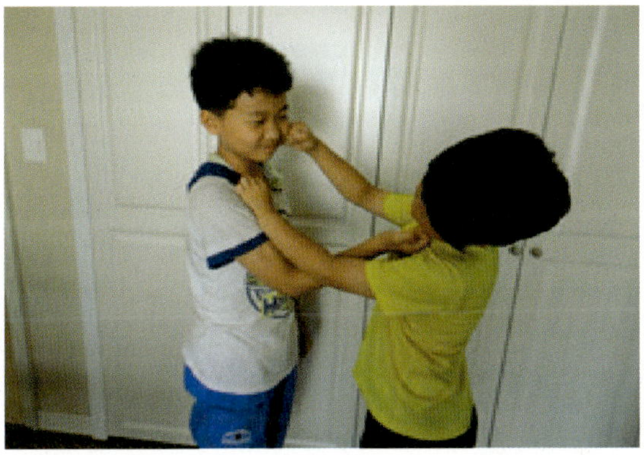

Sujin: When you say "Fighting!" you also use a certain hand gesture, right?
Chris: Right, in the U.S., we raise our fist in the air.
Sujin: In Korea we do that, too.
Chris: But we don't say "Fighting!" We say "**You can do it!**" "Fighting" means there's a conflict, an actual fight.

1. 한국인들은 "힘 내!" 또는 "힘내자!"라는 의미로 "파이팅/화이팅!"을 말하는데 사실 "파이팅/화이팅!"은 fighting에서 나온 단어로 "싸움"을 의미한다. 바른 표현으로는 go 또는 You/We can do it! 을 사용한다.

   A: Korea's leading by 2-0! (한국이 2-0으로 이기고 있어!)
   B: **Go** Korea! (한국 파이팅!)
   = **Let's go**, Korea! = Korea, **we can do it**!
   Korea fighting! (X)

2. Fighting은 fight에서 나온 단어로 fight은 "싸우다"를 기본의미로 해서 여러가지 상황에서 문맥에 맞게 사용될 수 있다.

   Several men **were fighting with** each other in the street.
   (몇 명의 남자들이 거리에서 서로 치고 받고 싸우고 있었다.)

   He **fought for** compensation for 3 years after the accident.
   (그는 사고 후 보상을 받기 위해 3년 동안 분투했다.)

   We will **fight (against)** terrorism for sure.
   (우리는 분명히 테러에 맞서 싸울 것이다.)

Lesson 11

MEN AND WOMEN COMMUNICATE DIFFERENTLY

CONTENTS

WARM UP

A. 아래 그림을 보고 질문에 답하시오.

1. Do you think that boys and girls tend to talk differently?
2. Do you think that men and women tend to talk differently?
3. Why do they seem to be different if they think and talk differently?

B. 대화를 듣고 T 또는 F를 고르시오.

Chris: Sujin, you look frustrated. What's wrong?
Sujin: Chris, why don't men ask for directions when they're clearly lost?
Chris: Well, for me, I know I can find my way if I just concentrate.
Sujin: Why are men like that? My husband never asks for help!
Chris: I guess it's because men are brought up that way.
Sujin: What do you mean?

1. Sujin is frustrated because she cannot drive well.	T	F
2. Chris asks for help when he gets lost.	T	F
3. Sujin's husband does not like to ask for directions.	T	F

vocabulary

directions (방향) concentrate (집중하다)
be/get lost (길을 잃다: I arrived there without being/getting lost.)
get lost! (꺼져!: He yelled at me, "Get lost!")
be brought up (양육되다, 자라나며 배우다)

VOCABULARY PREVIEW

A. 단어의 뜻과 표현을 공부해 보세요

1. intimate (매우 가까운) very close
several friends with whom I am intimate (나와 친한 몇 명의 친구들)

2. behave (행동하다) to act in a particular way
My dad sometimes behaves childishly. (내 아버지는 가끔 유치하게 행동하신다.)

3. ignore (무시하다) to pay no attention
You shouldn't ignore his advice. (그의 충고를 무시하면 안 된다.)

4. cooperative (협동, 협력하는) willing to help or do what people ask
cooperative employers (협력하는 직원들)

5. adult (성인의) fully grown or developed
An adult cat is an easy pet to take care of. (어른 애완용 고양이는 돌보는 것이 쉽다.)

6. annoyed (짜증이 나는, 약이 오른) a little angry
I was quite annoyed because he was late again!(나는 그가 또 늦었기 때문에 상당히 짜증이 났었다!)

7. indicate (나타내다, 표현하다) to show or point out
"Mr." indicates either a married or single man.("Mr."는 기혼남 또는 미혼남을 나타낸다.)

8. fascinating (대단히 흥미로운) very interesting
What a fascinating documentary! (대단히 흥미로운 다큐멘터리네요!)

9. professor (교수) a teacher at a university
I want to be a history professor. (나는 역사를 가르치는 교수가 되고 싶다.)

10. childhood (어린 시절) the time of being a child
I spent my childhood abroad. (나는 어린 시절을 외국에서 보냈다.)

B. 빈칸에 알맞은 표현을 넣으시오.

In contrast	learn about	are described as	compete with	For instance
(반대로)	(..에 대해 배우다)	(..로 묘사된다)	(..와 경쟁하다)	(예를 들면)

1. Jokingly, men and women ( ) coming from two different planets!
2. Boys normally play in large groups. ( ), girls play with a few close friends.
3. When boys play, they ( ) each other to be the leader of their group.
4. The topic of gender and language is really fascinating to ( ).
5. ( ), the pronoun, "he" was used to refer to either a man or woman.

LET'S READ IT TOGETHER

Men and Women Communicate Differently

1 "Men are from Mars, Women are from Venus" is a book by John Gray (1992). In his book, he explains that men and women think differently and so they speak differently. The differences are so great that these two groups are described as coming from two different planets! Many researchers have studied how gender differences are demonstrated in the English language in North American culture.

2 Deborah Tannen, a professor at an American university, explains that from early childhood boys and girls behave and speak differently. For example, when boys play, they compete with each other and try to become the leader of their group. In contrast, when girls play, they try to create rapport by creating a cooperative setting. This behavior is also seen in their language use. Boys often use authoritative language such as command forms, while girls tend to use more cooperative language that starts with "let's," for example.

compete

play

Quick Comprehension Questions

1. Who wrote "Men are from Mars, Women are from Venus"?
2. Who is Deborah Tannen?
3. Which group, boys or girls, values "equal status" more when playing?

vocabulary

Mars (화성)	Venus (금성)	researcher (연구자)
rapport (친밀감)	command (명령어)	authoritative (권위적인)

3. Gender differences are also maintained in adult conversations. Tannen found that when men hear complaints from women, the men try to offer solutions. However, when women talk about their problems, they prefer someone to just listen and share their feelings. This allows women to feel more intimate with others. Another example is when a woman asks a man if he would like to stop for coffee when driving, the man, considering his own preference, will instantly say "No, thanks." The woman may feel annoyed, thinking that her preference is being ignored. The man then will be confused about what he did wrong and get frustrated.

frustrated

4. On the issue of gender and language, researchers have also determined that there are gender-biased words in English, although there have been some efforts to neutralize them. For instance, in the past, the pronoun, "he" was used to refer to either a man or woman. Today "he or she" or "people" are more commonly used. Similarly, "man" could mean "people" previously, but now "people" or "human beings" are preferred. Moreover, in terms of identifying marital status, "Mr." can mean either a married or single man. Women, however, had to use either "Miss" or "Mrs." which are used to more specifically identify if they are married or not. These days, "Ms." is used to indicate either status for women, like Mr. Other gender-biased words include "chairman" and "businessman."

married

5. In short, the topic of gender and language seems to be really fascinating to learn about. If we understand how and why men and women think and speak differently, we will have better communication and much smoother relationships with the opposite sex.

Quick Comprehension Questions

1. In the past, how was "he" understood?
2. How is "Mr." understood?

vocabulary

complaint (불평)	solution (해결책)	instantly (즉시)
preference (선호)	identify (알아보다/확인하다)	chairman (회의의 의장)

READING COMPREHENSION

A. Understanding the Main Idea: 본문의 요지로 알맞은 것을 고르시오.

1. Ways of having better communication
2. Boys' and girls' different ways of playing
3. Gender-biased words in the English language
4. How gender differences are manifested in the English language

B. Text Organization

다음은 본문의 각 단락의 내용을 요약한 것으로, 어느 단락의 내용인지 그 단락의 번호를 적으시오.

P ______ To introduce the topic by mentioning the interesting title of a book

P _____ To illustrate how men and women differ in their conversational styles

P _____ To explain how boys and girls differ in their behavior and language use

P ______ To show how some English words are biased due to gender

P _______ To point out that understanding gender differences can enhance communication and relationships

C. Understanding Details:
아래의 문장이 본문의 내용과 맞으면 T, 틀리면 F를 선택하시오.

	True	False
1. Boys would say, "Let's take turns playing with the toy."		
2. Girls would say, "I will do this first."		
3. When men hear complaints from women, they feel that they need to offer solutions.		
4. Men would complain that women do not just say what they want.		
5. The address form of "Mr." does not indicate if a man is single or married.		
6. If a woman is married, the only possible address form is "Ms." before her last name.		

D. Reading Strategy

비교/대조의 전개 (Comparing and Contrasting)

비교란 둘 이상의 사람, 사물, 현상, 또는 사건들의 공통점을 열거, 서술하는 방식이고, 대조란 그 차이점을 열거, 서술하는 방식이다. 비교/대조의 전개구조는 특정 표시어구(signal words)를 찾아내면 쉽게 파악할 수 있다.

비교: like, similar to, similarly, also

대조: unlike, but, however, in contrast (to), while, on the other hand

비교 또는 대조의 전개구조를 나타내는 표시어구에 밑줄을 치시오.

1. For example, when boys play, they compete with each other and try to become the leader of their group. In contrast, when girls play, they try to create rapport by creating a cooperative setting.

2. For instance, in the past, the pronoun, "he" was used to refer to either a man or woman. Today "he or she" or "people" are more commonly used. Similarly, "man" could mean "people" previously, but now "people" or "human beings" are preferred.

VOCABULARY REVIEW

A. 빈칸에 알맞은 단어를 넣으시오.

identify describe behave cooperative annoyed fascinating rapport instantly

1. When doing a team project, it is best to be ( ).
2. I don't know her face. Can you ( ) her to me?
3. The film has such a ( ) storyline.
4. Some children ( ) very badly.
5. I get ( ) when people do not keep their word.
6. The teacher built up a good ( ) with the students.
7. To come up with a solution, we first need to ( ) what the problem is.
8. I was able to recognize her voice ( ).

B. Word Power

동사 + –(t)ion = 명사

접미사 –(t)ion을 붙이면 명사로 변하는 동사들이 있다. 하지만 그 변화과정에서 기본 동사의 철자가 탈락(예: cooperation)되거나 변하는 경우(예: competition)가 있기 때문에 주의해야 한다.

cooperate (협동, 협력하다) + –ion ⇨ cooperation (협동, 협력)
frustrate (좌절시키다, 불만스럽게 하다) + –ion ⇨ frustration (좌절, 불만)
negotiate (협상, 교섭하다) + –ion ⇨ negotiation (협상, 교섭)
compete (경쟁하다) + –tion ⇨ competition (경쟁)

1. We need your **cooperation** to successfully hold the event.
2. One of the best ways to deal with **frustration** is to exercise.
3. **Negotiation** is one of the most important skills in business.
4. Most boys hate losing in a **competition**.

GRAMMAR FOCUS

Indirect Questions (간접의문문)

직접의문문을 간접의문문으로 바꿔 말할 때, 어순의 변화가 있다. 직접의문문에서는 "의문사 + Be-동사 + 주어" 또는 "의문사 + 조동사 + 주어 + 일반동사" 이지만 간접의문문에서는 "의문사 + 주어 + Be-동사" 또는 "의문사 + 주어 + (조동사) + 일반동사" 의 형태가 된다.

직접의문문: **Why** (의문사) **do** (조동사) **men and women** (주어) **communicate** (일반동사) differently?

간접의문문: I wonder **why** (의문사) **men and women** (주어) **communicate** (일반동사) differently.

I wonder **why men and women communicate** differently.
Men wonder **what they did** wrong and get frustrated at women.

직접의문문	간접의문문
Men: "What did we do wrong?"	Men wonder what they did wrong.
Women: "Why don't men ask for directions?"	Women wonder why men do not ask for directions.
Children: "Why should we go to bed early?"	Children wonder why they should go to bed early.

A. 직접의문문을 간접의문문으로 바꾸시오.

1. "Why is Jane smiling?" ⇨ I wonder ( ).
2. "Who is that man?" ⇨ I wonder ( ).
3. "Why did you cry?" ⇨ Please tell me ( ).
4. "How did Tom get there?" ⇨ I asked ( ) there.

B. 다음 글을 읽고 틀린 부분을 찾아 맞게 고치시오.

I met an old friend last Sunday. We hadn't seen each other for a long time so we had a lot of questions for each other. He asked how was I doing and where was I living. He also asked what was my job. For me, I asked him if he was married. He said he was. I can't believe he's married and has children. In my eyes, he is still a little kid who I played with in my childhood.

LET'S TALK ABOUT IT

A. 다음 대화를 듣고 연습해 봅시다.

Chris: Sujin, I have a question for you.
Sujin: Sure, go ahead. I hope I can help.
Chris: Why can't women just say what they want to hear?
Sujin: Oh, I know where you're coming from.
Chris: I sometimes can't understand my wife, and what she really wants.
Sujin: It's true that we tend to be indirect when we speak.
Chris: **It seems like** when women say one thing, they mean something totally different.
Sujin: I think that's the difference between men and women. We tend to check how much others care about us without telling them what we want.

B. 유용한 표현들

1. "It seems like 절(주어 + 동사)"는 "–인 것 같다" 라는 추측의 표현이다. like대신 that도 사용 가능하다.

   It seems like you get happier as you get older.
   = **It seems that** you get happier as you get older.
   (당신은 나이가 들수록 더 행복해 지는 것 같군요.)

2. 같은 의미로 사용될 수 있는 다른 표현으로는 "It appears that 절(주어 + 동사)"이 있다. 하지만 It appears like는 가능하지 않다. I get the impression that도 가능하다.

   It appears that you get happier as you get older.
   = **I get the impression that** you get happier as you get older.
   (당신은 나이가 들수록 더 행복해 지는 것 같군요.)

   It appears like you get happier as you get older. (X)

C. 말해보기: 아래 빈칸에 알맞은 표현을 넣으시오.

1. A: Look Mom, aren't those Dad's shoes? (엄마, 저 신발 아빠 신발 아니예요?)
   B: ________________ your dad's already home. (아빠가 벌써 집에 오신 것 같구나.)
2. A: Look at the sky. (하늘 좀 봐봐.)
   B: ________________ it's going to rain soon. (곧 비가 올 것 같은데.)

Guy vs. Guys

Chris: Hey **guys,** why don't we order cheesecake, too?
Sujin: Guys? Don't you use the word for boys or men?
Chris: Yes, but we can also use it for a group of people, either men or women, or mixed.
Sujin: Oh, I didn't know that.

1. 단수형인 guy는 비격식체로 소년 또는 남자를 가리키지만, guy의 복수형인 guys는 여러 명의 남자들, 여자들, 또는 남녀 상관없이 무리 지어 있는 사람들을 가리킨다.

   친구가 다른 친구에게: Dave's **a cool guy**. (데이브는 멋진 녀석이야.)
   어머니가 자녀들에게: **Guys,** what do you want for dinner?
   (얘들아, 저녁으로 뭘 먹고 싶니?)

2. Guy와 비슷한 형태로 gay란 단어가 있는데 "동성애자의(특히 남자)"를 의미하는 형용사로 사용된다. Guy의 철자와 비슷하기 때문에 주의가 필요하다. 참고로 여자 동성애자를 표현하고 싶을 때는 lesbian을 쓰면 된다. 이 때, lesbian은 gay와는 다르게 명사, 형용사 모두 사용이 가능하다.

   Dave's **gay**. (데이브는 동성애자야.) Dave's **a gay man**.
   Dave's **a gay**. (X)
   Ann is **(a) lesbian**. (앤은 동성애자야.)

Lesson 12
A FOREIGNER'S EXPERIENCES IN KOREA

CONTENTS

Reading: 외국인의 한국 문화 체험기

Reading Strategy: 사실과 의견 구별하기

Word Power: sleep과 관련된 말뭉치

Grammar Focus: 형용사로 사용되는 분사

Let's Talk About It: 여행장소에서 할 수 있는 것들 추천

Common Errors in English: Today morning vs. This morning

WARM UP

A. 아래 그림을 보고 질문에 답하시오

1. Which place do you like to recommend to foreigners?
2. Why do you like to recommend that place?
3. Which place do you think they like most?

B. 대화를 듣고 질문에 답하시오

Karen: I heard that I need to be aware of Korean table manners. What are they?

Sujin: Let's see… you should wait until the eldest person begins eating to start your meal.

Karen: Wow, I didn't know that.

Sujin: And you should try to pace yourself so that you can finish your meal around the same time everyone else does.

Karen: So I should try to talk less and focus on my meal, right?

Sujin: Well, I wouldn't worry too much about talking too much, just go with the flow.

1. Karen and Sujin are talking about Korean food. T F
2. Sujin told Karen that she has to be the first one to begin eating. T F
3. Sujin advised Karen to talk a lot when eating her meal. T F

vocabulary

be aware of ~ (~에 대해 알다) table manners (식탁예절)
the eldest person (최고 연장자) pace yourself (속도를 조절한다)
around the same time (거의 같은 시간에) focus on ~ (~에 집중한다)
go with the flow (흐름을 따르다)

VOCABULARY PREVIEW

A. 단어의 뜻과 표현을 공부해 보시오.

1. worried (걱정이 된) unhappy to think about problems
I am worried about your health. (당신의 건강이 걱정이다.)

2. aspect (양상) one of the parts of its nature
Talk about every aspect of it. (전부 다 얘기해 주세요.)

3. allow (허용한다) to give permission to do it
I don't allow looking elsewhere in class. (나는 수업 중 딴청 하는 것을 허용하지 않는다.)

4. noise (소음) a loud or unpleasant sound
A strange noise broke his sleep. (이상한 소리에 그는 잠이 깼다.)

5. face (~를 향한다) to be looking in a particular
The hotel faces the sea. (그 호텔은 바다를 향하고 있다.)

6. admit (인정한다) to accept something as true
I admit what I said before was wrong. (내가 전에 말한 게 틀렸다고 인정한다.)

7. assume (~라고 생각한다) to imagine something is true
I assume it just means nothing. (난 이게 별거 아니라고 생각해.)

8. merchant (상인) a person who buys or sells goods
The merchant has a large staff of clerk. (그 상인은 많은 점원을 거느리고 있다.)

9. additional (부가의) extra things
I paid additional charge. (나는 추가요금을 지불했다.)

10. stroll (산책) to walk in a slow, relaxed way
It's fun to take a stroll with a dog. (강아지와 산책을 하는 것은 즐겁다.)

B. 빈칸에 알맞은 표현을 넣으시오.

am used to (−에 익숙한다)	are different from (−와 다른)	as soon as (−하자마자)	burst into laughter (웃음을 터트리다)	for free (공짜로)

1. I ( ) the street markets in my home country.
2. ( ) I stepped into the market, I saw a hanbok shop.
3. Everyone around me ( ).
4. The merchant gave me additional helpings ( ).
5. Korean street markets ( ) what I expected.

LET'S READ IT TOGETHER

A Foreigner's Experiences in Korea

1 Every year more and more foreigners travel to Korea to visit, work, or stay. Many of them share their experiences about Korea by using blogs. Jennifer is one of these people.

Hanok Stay

2 Last weekend, I travelled to Jeonju and stayed at a hanok. I was a bit worried about sleeping on the hard floor at first, but I actually slept soundly and my back was fine in the morning. I found several amazing aspects of the hanok. First of all, the floor was nicely heated via "Ondol", a traditional stone floor that is heated by fire and covered over by wooden panels. The windows were made of Korean traditional paper which allowed for more air flow, so the air was fresh in the room. The walls were made of mud and fairly thick, so I didn't hear any noise even though my room was on the ground floor facing the street. In the morning, my host served a typical Jeonju breakfast with doenjang chiggae, a kind of boiling hot soybean paste stew, grilled mackerel, and many side dishes. For me, it was certainly a unique experience because I'm just a coffee-for-breakfast type of person back in the U.S. However, I have to admit that while it was great for two nights, I was happy to get back to my own bed on my return home.

Ondol

wooden panel

mud

Quick Comprehension Questions

1. How does Jennifer share her experiences about Korea?
2. Why didn't she hear any noise while sleeping in the hanok?
3. How many nights did she stay at the hanok ?

vocabulary

a bit(약간) sleep soundly(푹 자다) back(등, 뒤에) amazing(놀라운)
flow(흐름) mud(진흙) thick(두꺼운) ground floor(일층)
a coffee-for-breakfast type of person(커피를 아침 삼아 먹는 사람)
on my return home(집으로 돌아와서)

Kwangjang Market

3 Today, I visited Kwangjang Market. It was my first visit to a real Korean street market. Since I am used to the street markets in my home country, I assumed they would be similar in Korea. But I found that Korean street markets are quite different from what I expected.

4 As soon as I stepped into the market, I was surprised to see a lot of different sections such as the hanbok section, an area for agricultural and marine products, and a section for fabric. What I liked most was a lot of the stalls selling fresh fish, vegetables, rice cakes, kimbap and so on. They looked and smelled so delicious that I couldn't stop trying the different kinds. They were really tasty and furthermore incredibly cheap; A bowl of delicious red bean porridge was only 4,000 won, about half the price in normal restaurants. And the merchant gave me additional helpings for free. By the time I had finished, I was so full that I could hardly breathe!

5 Later while I was looking around in a hanbok shop, the people there allowed me to try on a beautiful hanbok. When I looked in the mirror, I thought the costume made me look like an angel. I was so excited that I tried to do a Korean traditional bow on the floor. But I fell over, and everyone around me burst into laughter. I was a little embarrassed but it was Ok. It was a fun and interesting stroll through the place where unique aspects of Korean culture can be experienced.

stall

fabric

Red bean porridge

Quick Comprehension Questions

1. What did she assume about Korean street markets?
2. What did she like most?
3. Why did everyone around her burst into laughter?

vocabulary

similar(비슷한) step into(~로 걸어 들어가다) section(구획, 부분)
agricultural(농업의) marine products(해산물) incredibly(믿기 힘들게)
bowl(그릇, 사발) hardly(거의~ 않는) helping(한 사람 몫의 음식)
breathe(숨쉬다) looked in the mirror(거울을 들여다보다) laughter(웃음)
costume embarrassed (당황한) stroll(산책)

READING COMPREHENSION

A. Understanding the Main Idea: 본문의 요지로 알맞은 것을 고르시오.

1. A foreigner's recommendation about Korea
2. A foreigner's experiences with real Korean life
3. A foreigner s viewpoint on Korean street market
4. A foreigner's analysis of the amazing aspects of hanok

B. Text Organization: 제니퍼의 여행기를 읽고 다음의 빈칸을 알맞은 말로 채우시오.

1. Hanok Stay: 한옥의 장점과 이로 인한 효과

Aspects	Effects
◈The floor is ________________.	→ The room was warm.
◈The windows allow for ____________.	→ The air was ______.
◈The walls were made of ______ and ______.	→ She didn't ________.

2. Kwangjang Market: 제니퍼의 한국 시장에 대한 예상과 실제 한국 시장 특유의 양상

Jennifer's assumption :

- Korean street markets would be ________ to those in her home country.

Unique aspects of Korean street market :

- There were ____________________ in the market.
- Foods were very ________, and prices were incredibly ________.
- The merchant gave her additional ________.
- The hanbok she tried on was so ________ that it made her ________.

C. Understanding Details:

아래의 문장이 본문의 내용과 맞으면 T, 틀리면 F를 선택하시오.

	True	False
1. Jennifer slept well but her back was hurting in the morning.		
2. The air was fresh in the room because the walls were made of mud.		
3. Jennifer had simple breakfast when she was in the U.S.		
4. Foods were delicious and very cheap in the market.		
5. Jennifer paid for additional helpings of red bean porridge.		
6. Jennifer tried a beautiful hanbok and bought it.		

D. Reading Strategy

사실과 의견 구별하기 (Distinguishing Facts and Opinions)

사실과 의견이 혼합된 글에서 이 둘을 정확히 구별해야 글을 더 잘 이해하고 주어진 정보를 정확히 평가할 수 있습니다. 사실은 실제로 일어난 누구나 일반적으로 그렇다고 인정하는 것인 반면, 의견은 개인의 생각이나 감정이 개입된 주관적인 내용으로 다른 사람이 동의하지 않을 수도 있다. 의견을 나타내는 문장에는 감정 형용사(**happy, amazing, interesting**)나 의견을 나타내는 표현(**I think, I assume, For me**)이 들어 있다. 다음 두 문장은 사실과 의견의 차이를 잘 보여준다.

사실: It was a two-hour- long stroll. (두 시간 걸린 산책이었다.)
의견: It was a fun and interesting stroll.(재밌고 흥미로운 산책이었다.)

아래 문장을 읽고 사실이면 (F) 를 의견이면 (O) 를 빈칸에 쓰시오.

1. Last weekend, I travelled to Jeonju and stayed at a hanok. (   )
2. The merchant gave me additional helpings for free. (   )
3. For me, it was certainly a unique experience. (   )
4. It was my first visit to a real Korean street market. (   )
5. I assumed they would be similar in Korea. (   )
6. The windows were made of Korean traditional paper which allowed for more air flow. (   )

VOCABULARY REVIEW

A. 빈칸에 알맞은 단어를 넣으시오.

allow	worried	stroll	admits	faces	assume	noise	additional

1. Many Korean students are __________ about the new test.
2. The supervisors __________ two weeks' vacation after three years.
3. I can't hear anything because of the __________ in the factory.
4. The window in my room __________ west.
5. My husband never __________ that he was wrong.
6. I __________ this ring is the most expensive one in this shop.
7. There will be a small __________ charge for the service.
8. On Sunday, you can see thousands people __________ along the beach.

B. Word Power

sleep과 관련된 말뭉치

영어에서는 두 개 또는 그 이상의 단어들이 반드시 함께 쓰는 경우가 많은 데 이를 말뭉치(**collocation**)이라고 한다. 예를 들어 '푹 자다"라는 말은 'sleep deeply'라고 하지 않고 '**sleep soundly**' 또는 '**sleep well**'이라고 한다.

한국어 표현	Collocated Expressions
잘 자다	sleep well/soundly
잠자리에 들다	go to sleep/bed
잠이 들다	fall asleep
충분히 자다	get enough sleep
자지 않고 지내다	go without sleep

1. What time usually do you go _________ sleep?(보통 몇 시에 잠자리에 드나요?)
2. How long does it take you to _________ asleep?(잠드는 데 얼마나 걸리나요?)
3. How long can you go _________ sleep? (잠 안자고 얼마나 버틸 수 있나요?)
4. Did you _________ enough sleep last night? (어제 밤에 충분히 잤나요?)
5. Do you sleep _________ every night? (매일 밤 잘 자나요?)

GRAMMAR FOCUS

Participles as Adjective (형용사로 쓰이는 분사)

동사 과거분사나 현재 분사는 형용사처럼 사용되어 명사를 직접 꾸며주거나 보어의 역할을 한다. 과거 분사는 주로 사람의 감정을 묘사하기 위해 사용되고, 과거분사는 그런 감정을 불러 일으키는 사물이나 상황을 묘사하기 위해 사용된다.

- I'm **surprised** to see you here. : a **surprised** student (놀란 학생)
- They told us some **surprising** news.: a **surprising** news (놀라운 소식)

현재진행형 (사물, 상황)	과거 분사 (사람)
The party is **boring**: a **boring** party	The girl was **bored** at the party: a **bored** girl
The news was **shocking**: a **shocking** news	The man was **shocked** by the news: a **shocked** man
The movie is **exciting**: a **exciting** movie	The baby is **excited** about the movie: a **excited** baby
The book was **amazing**: an **amazing** book	The boys were **amazed** by the book: **amazed** boys

Be careful: 현재 분사도 사람을 꾸며줄 수 있다. 이 경우에는 "~하게 만드는' 정도의 뜻이다.

He's a boring speaker.(지루하게 만드는 연사)
She is an amazing professor. (대단한 교수)

A. 주어진 단어를 적절한 분사형으로 변형하여 각 문장을 완성하시오.

1. surprise: It was (surprising) news. Everyone was (surprised).
2. bore: What a ( ) class! I was completely ( ).
3. interest: He's ( ) in magic. Magic is very ( ) to him.
4. excite: I'm ( ) about my vacation. It's going to be ( ).
5. tire: I'm ( ). Today was a ( ) day.

B. 다음 글을 읽고 틀린 부분을 찾아 맞게 고치시오.

Chris has an amazed personality. He knows how to cheer people up. For example, whenever the meeting is bored, he tells interested stories that get everyone involved in the discussion again. We are all very exciting to work with Chris.

LET'S TALK ABOUT IT

A. 다음 대화를 듣고 연습해 봅시다

Sofia: I'm going to Busan next week. **What should I see there**?

Hansol: **You should definitely** visit Haeundae Beach.

Sofia: **What can I do there**?

Hansol: There's a lot to do. You can swim, play in the water, go banana boating, do some jet skiing, or just work on your suntan.

Sofia: And **what else**?

Hansol: Oh, **you shouldn't miss** Jagalchi Fish Market. You can have the best seafood there!

B. 유용한 표현들

1. 여러분이 어딘가 처음 방문하는 곳에서 뭘 보거나 해야 할 지 궁금할 때 **What should I see there?** (거기서 뭘 봐야 해?) 혹은 **What can I do there?** (거기서 뭘 할 수 있어?)라고 물어 볼 수 있다.
2. You should definitely visit Haeundae Beach.(해운대에 반드시 가는 게 좋아)라는 대답에서 "**should**"는 "~를 해야 한다"는 의무(must)의 뜻이 아니라 "~하는 게 좋아"라는 권유의 뜻이다. 예를 들어 I feel sick.(나 아픈 것 같아)라는 말에 대한 다음 두 답을 보면 should의 뜻이 분명해 질 것이다.

   - You **should** go see a doctor.(병원에 가보는 게 좋겠어): 권유
   - You **must** go see a doctor. (병원에 가야 해): 의무

3. **What else?**는 **What else should I see there?** (거기서 뭘 봐야 해?) 혹은 What else can I do there?의 준말로서 "그 밖에 또 뭐가 있어?"라는 뜻이다.
4. **You shouldn't miss** ~ 에서 miss는 "놓치다, 빼먹다"라는 뜻으로 "~을 빼먹어서는 안돼"라는 뜻으로 **You should definitely** ~ (반드시~해야 돼)와 거의 같은 뜻이다.

C. 말해보기: 아래 빈칸에 알맞은 표현을 넣으시오.

1. A: I'm going to Paris this summer. ____________________?
   (이번 여름에 파리 가는데 거기서 뭘 봐야 하지?)
   B: You ______________visit the Louvre museum. (루브르 미술관에 꼭 가야 해.)
2. A: What else? (그 밖에 또 뭐가 있지?)
   B: Oh, you ______________________ Eiffel Tower. (에펠탑을 빼 먹어서는 안돼.)

COMMON ERRORS IN ENGLISH

Today morning vs. This morning

Karen: Sujin, when is your job interview?
Sujin: **Today morning**.
Karen: Wow, you mean **this morning**? Well, good luck.
Sujin: Oh Yea, this morning. Thanks. See you **this night**, Karen.
Karen: See you **tonight**!!

1. '오늘 아침'이란 표현을 할 때 한국말을 그대로 옮겨 today morning이라고 하는 경우가 있는데 뜻은 이해할 수 있지만 어색한 표현이다. 맞는 표현은 **this morning**이다.

2. 그러면 오늘 오후, 오늘 밤, 오늘 저녁, 어제 밤은 뭐라고 할까요.
   오늘 오후: today afternoon (X) ⇨ **this afternoon** (O)
   오늘 저녁: today night (X) ⇨ **this evening** (O)
   오늘 밤: today night (X), this night(X) ⇨ **tonight** (O)
   어제 밤: yesterday night (X) ⇨ **last night** (O)

3. 그런데 아침에, 오후에, 저녁에, 밤에는 전치사를 사용하여 약간 다르게 표현한다.
   아침에: **in the morning** 오후에: **in the afternoon**
   저녁에: **in the evening** 밤에: **at night**
   - I get up early in the morning. (나는 아침에 일찍 일어난다.)

4. 오늘 아침에, 오늘 오후에, 오늘 밤에,는 전치사를 사용하지 않는다.
   오늘 아침에: in this morning (X) ⇨ **this morning** (O)
   오늘 오후에: in this afternoon (X) ⇨ **this afternoon** (O)
   오늘 저녁에: in this evening (X) ⇨ **this evening** (O)
   오늘 밤에: at tonight (X) ⇨ **tonight** (O)
   - I got up early this morning. (나는 오늘 아침에 일찍 일어났다.)
     시간을 나타내는 표현들은 한국식 사고와 다른 점이 많으므로 표현을 정확히 익혀 두어야 한다.

Lesson 13
HOLIDAYS AROUND THE WORLD

CONTENTS

Reading: 세계 여러 나라의 축제일

Reading Strategy: 이야기의 전개 순서 파악하기

Word Power: 명사와 동사의 형태가 같은 단어들

Grammar Focus: 주어와 동사의 일치

Let's Talk About It: 간접적으로 의견 제시

Common Errors in English: Congratulation on your birthday vs. Happy birthday

WARM UP

A. 아래 그림을 보고 질문에 답하시오.

Losar (Tibet)

Republic Day (Niger)

1. What do you think they are celebrating in these pictures?
2. What are some clues that helped you in the pictures?
3. Are there any similar celebrations in Korea?

B. 대화를 듣고 질문에 답하시오.

Minho: Hi, Karen, how was your trip to Dubai?
Karen: Well, I went during Ramadan, so it was kind of difficult to have lunch because the restaurants were closed.
Minho: What is Ramadan?
Karen: It's a period when Muslims don't eat anything during the day.
Minho: Wow, I've never heard of that tradition.
Karen: I didn't know about it either. But they served a big meal after 7 so it was all right.

1. It was easy for Karen to have lunch in Dubai.	T	F
2. Minho was not aware of Ramadan.	T	F
3. Karen could have dinner after 7 in the evening.	T	F

vocabulary

Ramadan (이슬람교에서의 단식기간)　have lunch (점심을 먹다.)
I've never heard of ~ (~에 대해 들어 본 적이 없다)
I didn't know about it either (그것에 대해서는 나도 역시 몰라)
either (부정문에서 '역시'라는 뜻)
served a big meal (성대한 식사를 제공하다)

VOCABULARY PREVIEW

A. 단어의 뜻과 표현을 공부해 보세요.

1. ancestor (조상) any member of your family from long ago
His ancestors came from China. (그의 조상은 중국에서 왔다.)

2. decorate (장식하다) to add something to make it more attractive
He decorated the table with flowers. (그는 꽃으로 테이블을 장식했다.)

3. relative (친척) a person connected with others by blood
She is a relative of mine. (그녀는 나의 친척이다.)

4. last (지속하다) to continue for some period
The party lasted six hours. (그 잔치는 여섯 시간 동안 지속되었다.)

5. gather (모이다) to come together in one place
Let's gather round the fire and sing. (불가에 모여서 노래하자)

6. custom (풍습) something done traditionally in a society
This custom is very old. (이 풍속은 매우 오래되었다.)

7. attend (참여하다) to be at an event or go to a place
She couldn't attend the meeting. (그녀는 그 모임에 참석할 수 없었다.)

8. bless for (축복하다) God to protect or help someone
God bless you and your family. (당신과 당신 가족에 축복이 있길!)

9. pray (기도하다) to speak to God to ask for help
We will pray for you. (우리는 너를 위해 기도할 것이다.)

10. remove (제거하다) to take something away
Remove the shells from these peanuts. (땅콩 껍질을 제거해라.)

B. 빈칸에 알맞은 표현을 넣으시오.

At first glance	get together	dress up in	gave out	light up
(첫눈에는)	(모이다)	(차려 입다)	(나누어 주다)	(불을 밝히다)

1. Families ( ) and prepare their ancestors' favorite food.
2. The Hindus ( ) their houses with lamps or candles.
3. The King of Spain ( ) grapes to all of his people on New Year's Eve.
4. ( ), the Day of the Dead may sound like a sad occasion.
5. People ( ) masks and costumes.

LET'S READ IT TOGETHER

Holidays around the World

1 Every culture has its own unique way of celebrating special days. Here are some descriptions of different celebrations around the world.

grave

candle

mask

the Day of the Dead in Mexico

2 At first glance, the Day of the Dead may sound like a sad occasion, but it is actually a celebration in Mexico. This happy family event lasts for three days between October 31st and November 2nd. During this period, Mexicans take time to remember and honor their ancestors. On the first day, families visit the graves of their deceased relatives. They decorate the gravesite with flowers, earth, and candles. On the second day, families get together and cook their ancestors' favorite food. In some places, people spend the whole night at the grave. During the night, they have a party, share food, play music, talk, and drink. On the last day, the entire town joins in on this celebration where people dress up in masks and costumes and attend parades. There are even costume contests. This celebration originally began as a day of giving thanks for the year's harvest. Now it is a time of remembrance and celebration.

Quick Comprehension Questions

1. How long does the Day of the Dead celebration last?
2. What is the purpose of the Day of the Dead celebration?
3. Where do some people spend the whole night?

vocabulary

celebration(축하행사) occasion(행사) take time to ~ (~을 시간을 들여 하다)
honor(찬양하다) deceased(사망한) originally(원래)
harvest(추수) remembrance(추모)

New Year's Day in Spain

3 The people of Spain have a custom to eat 12 grapes at midnight on New Year's Day, one grape for each stroke of the clock. They believe that each grape represents a month of the year. Each sweet grape they eat will be a good month and each sour one will be a bad month. For example, if the second grape is sour, then February, the second month, will be an unlucky month. Thus, they hope all the grapes will be sweet. They also try to eat all the grapes before the 12th chime because of the belief that this will give them good luck for the New Year. This custom started in 1909 to celebrate the big grape harvest in Spain. The King of Spain gave out grapes to all of his people on New Year's Eve.

12 grapes

clock

harvest

the Festival of Lights in India

4 Diwali or the Festival of Lights is one of the most important holidays of the Hindus. It is celebrated during the last two days and the first two days of the Hindu lunar month (September to October). The Hindus light up their houses with lamps or candles to receive Lakshmi, the goddess of wealth. They believe that during this time the goddess returns from her country home and uses the lamps to help guide her way. People pray for Lakshmi to bring them good fortune and believe she will not bless a house that is not lit up. Diwali is also the beginning of the Hindu New Year. To welcome the start of the New Year, people clean their houses, invite their friends and relatives, and encourage each other to remove anger, hate, and jealousy from their lives.

Quick Comprehension Questions

1. Why do the Spanish people try to eat all the grapes before the 12th chime?
2. When is the Festival of Lights celebrated?
3. Who is Lakshmi?

vocabulary

stroke(시계 종이 치는 것) sour(맛이 신) chime(종소리) lunar month(음력) goddess(여신) wealth(부) guide(안내하다) fortune(행운) anger(분노) hate(증오) jealousy(질투)

READING COMPREHENSION

A. Understanding the Main Idea: 본문의 요지로 알맞은 것을 고르시오.

1. Understanding new year's eve traditions around the world
2. Understanding the similarities of celebrations around the world
3. Understanding different celebrations around the world
4. Understanding the history of celebrations around the world

B. Text Organization

본문 내용을 기반으로 아래에 제시된 표를 완성하여 두 축제를 비교해 보시오.

Name	the Day of the Dead	the Festival of Lights
Where	______	______
When	______	______
Purpose	to remember and honor ______	To honor the goddess of wealth and to welcome ______
Activities	■ visit the graves of their ______ ■ decorate the gravesite with ______ ■ spend the whole night at the grave ■ prepare ______ and have a party ■ dress up in ______	■ ______ their houses ■ ______ their houses with lamps or candles ■ pray for Lakshmi to bring them ______ ■ encourage each other to remove ______ from their lives

C. Understanding Details:
아래의 문장이 본문의 내용과 맞으면 T, 틀리면 F를 선택하시오.

	True	False
1. The Day of the Dead is a happy celebration in Mexico.		
2. All the Mexican people spend the whole night at the grave during the festival.		
3. Spanish people believe that if the second grape is sour, March will be a lucky month.		
4. Spanish people try to eat all the grapes because they are sweet.		
5. The Hindus believe that Lakshmi will bless a house that is not lit up.		
6. Diwali is the last day of the Hindu New Year.		

D. Reading Strategy

개요를 통해 글 정리하기 (Organizing Thoughts when Reading)

개요는 글의 구조를 식별하고 중심 내용을 쉽게 알 수 있게 해 줍니다. 글을 읽고 개요를 작성할 때는 아래 사항에 유의합니다:

1) 개요의 틀은 본문의 틀과 같도록 합니다.
2) 본문의 핵심 내용을 간결하게 정리합니다.
3) 목록 형식으로 나열하여 전체 요지가 드러나게 합니다.

아래 글을 읽고 개요를 완성하시오.

Mardi Gras is a popular American holiday in New Orleans, Louisiana. People in New Orleans started to celebrate Mardi Gras in the 1700s. The celebration of Mardi Gras last for several weeks in the early part of the year. During the period, there are over 60 parades. People join the parades and throw things, such as necklaces, false money and clothes, to the people in the street. The people in the street try to catch as many items as they can. Mardi Gras is a very exciting event for everyone.

- Mardi Gras is a popular __________ in __________.
- It started to be celebrated in __________.
- It lasts for __________ in __________.
- There are __________ parades.
- In the parades, people throw __________ and __________ to the people in the street.

VOCABULARY REVIEW

A. 빈칸에 알맞은 단어를 넣으시오.

remove pray blessed custom decorate attend ancestors last

1. Koreans visit graves of their ____________ on Chuseok.
2. Will you help me ____________ the Christmas tree with lights?
3. The batteries ____________ about 10 hours and are rechargeable.
4. The British have the ____________ of drinking tea at four o'clock.
5. Didn't you ____________ Springfield Junior High?
6. May you be ____________ in the Name of Father, and of the Son, and of the Holy Spirit.
7. Our Father in heaven, we __________ that your name will always be kept holy.
8. I would like ____________ the stain from the shirts.

B. Word Power

명사와 동사의 형태가 같은 단어들

영어에서는 명사와 동사로 동시에 사용이 가능한 단어들이 많이 있습니다. 그 단어가 명사인지 동사인지는 문장 안에서 그 단어가 어떻게 사용되었느냐에 따라 결정됩니다.

	명사	동사		명사	동사
sound	소리	(소리가) 들리다	return	귀환	돌아오다
light	빛	불을 켜다	hope	희망	희망하다
guide	안내자	안내하다	cook	요리사	요리하다
start	시작	시작하다	drink	음료수	마시다
hate	미움	미워하다	smell	냄새	(냄새를) 맡다

1. I will not **drink** that strange red **drink**.
   (나는 저 이상한 빨간 색 음료를 안 마실 거다.)
2. "I will **cook** you your favorite meal," said the **cook**.
   ("네가 좋아하는 요리를 해 줄게"라고 요리사가 말했다.)
3. Everyone began to **laugh**, and it was the loudest **laugh** I'd ever heard.
   (모든 사람이 웃었다. 그건 여태 내가 들어본 가장 큰 웃음소리였다.)
4. I could **smell** sweet **smell** from the restaurant.
   (나는 그 식당에서 나는 맛있는 냄새를 맡을 수 있었다.)

GRAMMAR FOCUS

Subject-Verb agreement (주어와 동사의 일치)

현재 시제의 문장에서 주어가 3인칭 단수일 경우 동사의 원형에 반드시 -(e)s를 붙여야 한다. 주어로 사용된 명사가 단수인지 복수인지를 정확히 파악해야 한다.

The entire **town** joins in on this celebration.
Mexicans take time to remember and honor their ancestors.
Every culture **has** its own unique way of celebrating special days.
Each grape represent**s** a month of the year.
People pray for Lakshmi to bring them good fortune.

Singular (단수)	Plural (복수)
▪ Every +명사: Every culture ▪ Each + 명사: Each student ▪ everyone, information, money, milk	▪ 명사+s: grapes ▪ 단수명사 and 단수명사: Tom and Jane ▪ people, children

Be careful: There is/are의 경우에는 주어가 뒤에 온다는 점에 유의해야 한다.
There **are** even costume contest**s**.
There **is** a lot of **information** on the internet about the festival.

A. 알맞은 단어를 선택하여 문장을 완성하시오.

1. Karen (speak/speaks) Korean very well.
2. My brother and sister (live/lives) in Seoul.
3. There (is/are) many children waiting for New Year's Eve.
4. Everyone (enjoy/enjoys) the party.
5. My children (love/loves) to swim.

B. 다음 글을 읽고 틀린 부분을 찾아 맞게 고치시오.

On the last day of the year, the people of Spain gets together with their friends and wait until midnight. Everyone have twelve grapes ready to eat at midnight. When the clock start to chime, people put a grape in their mouth, one grape for each stroke of the clock. When the chiming end, all the people has a mouthful of grapes.

LET'S TALK ABOUT IT

A. 다음 대화를 듣고 연습해 봅시다.

Sujin: **I heard that** you were in Spain last month.
Chris: Yeah, I went to experience the Tomato Festival.
Sujin: **Is it true** the people throw tomatoes at each other during the festival?
Chris: Yeah, it was a really amazing experience.
Sujin: Really? **I'm not sure if** I like the idea of wasting food like that.
Chris: Well, it just happens once a year.
Sujin: Yeah, but they waste tons of tomatoes. I think it's just too much.
Chris: It's just harmless fun. **Don't take it so seriously**, Sofia.

B. 유용한 표현들: 소원, 기원하기

1. **I heard that~(~라는 말을 들었는데), Is it true~(~사실이야?)**, 의 표현 사용하면 간접적으로 좀 더 세련되고 부드럽게 의견을 전달할 수 있다. 첫 문장은 직접적인 표현은 **Were you in Spain last month?** (지난 달에 스페인에 갔었니?) **Do the people throw tomatoes at each other during the festival?** (사람들이 축제기간 동안 서로에게 토마토를 던지니?)이다.
2. **I'm not sure if(~에 대해 확신이 안 들어)**라는 말 역시 그 직접적인 뜻은 **I don't like** the idea of wasting food like that.(나는 음식을 낭비하는 것이 마음에 안 들어)인데 이를 간접적으로 표현할 때 쓰인다.
3. **Don't take it so seriously.**는 어떤 일에 대해 **I think it's just too much.**(너무 지나친 것 같아)라는 반응을 보일 때 '너무 심각하게 받아들이지 마'라고 충고할 때 쓰는 표현이다.
4. **It just happens once a year.** (그건 단지 일년에 한 번 벌어져).에서 once a year는 일년에 한 번이라는 뜻으로 twice a year(일년에 두 번), three times a year(일년에 세 번)등도 알아둘 필요가 있다.

C. 말해보기: 아래 빈칸에 알맞은 표현을 넣으시오.

1. A: ____________ people spend the whole night at the grave during the Days of the Dead? (죽은 이들의 날에 사람들이 무덤에서 밤을 새는 것이 사실이야?)
   B: Yeah, it is a really amazing tradition. (그래, 그건 정말 놀라운 전통이야)
2. A: Jason made fun of my name. I think it's just too much.
   (제이슨이 내 이름을 가지고 놀렸어. 너무 지나친 것 같아.)
   B: ________________________. (너무 심각하게 받아들이지 마)

Congratulation on your birthday vs. Happy birthday

Minho: I'm going to graduate next month.
Chris: **Congratulations**! I knew you could do it.
Minho: Thank you Chris. I'm really excited. By the way, isn't your birthday tomorrow?
Chris: Yes, how did you know that?
Minho: You told me before. **Congratulation on your birthday**.
Chris: Uh…Uhh.. thank you.

1. 이 대화에서 민호는 두 가지 실수를 했다. 첫째, Congratulation은 항상 복수형인 Congratulations라고 해야 하는데 단수형을 썼다. 또한 생일 축하 인사는 보통 Happy birthday.라고 하는데 Congratulation on your birthday.라고 말했다. 그리고 크리스의 생일은 내일인데 미리 축하를 하고 있고 있는 데 이런 경우 미국에서는 **Happy birthday in advance** (미리 생일 축하해)라고 흔히 말한다. 이메일로 뭔가를 부탁하면서 아직 상대방의 답을 받지 않은 상황에서 먼저 감사의 인사부터 하는 경우가 있다. 이럴 때에는 **Thank you in advance** 라고 하면 된다.

2. Congratulations는 어떤 사람이 노력을 기울여 뭔가를 성취한 것을 축하할 때 사용되는 말이기 때문에, 만일 Congratulations on your birthday라고 말하면 **'정말 이렇게 생일을 맞이 할 줄 몰랐는데 정말 노력하여 생일을 맞이하게 되어 축하한다'**는 의미를 가지게 되어 한 백 살쯤 된 노인에게는 쓸 수 있을 지 모르지만 일반적으로는 어색한 표현이 되는 것이다.

Lesson 14
THE KOREAN WAVE: PAST, PRESENT AND FUTURE

CONTENTS

WARM UP

A. 아래 그림을 보고 질문에 답하시오

1. Which TV drama do you like most?
2. Which one do you like to recommend to foreigners?
3. Why do you like to recommend it?

B. 대화를 듣고 질문에 답하시오

Chris: While I was in Thailand, I was surprised to see so many people watching Korean TV programs.

Minho: Really? That's amazing.

Chris: Yeah, and a lot of people were interested in learning about Korean language and culture, too.

Minho: I really think the Korean Wave has made more people aware of and interested in Korean culture all over the world.

Chris: How did this all begin with?

Minho: It all started with a Korean TV drama titled "Winter Sonata."

1. Chris was surprised to see that Korean T.V programs were popular in Thailand. T F

2. Minho thinks that books made Korean culture known all over the world. T F

3. The Korean Wave started in Thailand. T F

vocabulary

watch TV (텔레비전을 보다) the Korean Wave (한류)
aware of~ (~에 대해 아는) started with ~ (~로 시작하다)
titled ~ (~라는 제목의)
made Korean culture known (한국 문화를 알려지게 만들다)

VOCABULARY PREVIEW

A. 단어의 뜻과 표현을 공부해 보시오.

1. spread (널리 알려지다) to cause to be widely known
The rumor have spread over the village. (그 소문은 동네방네 알려졌다.)

2. Include (포함하다) to have something smaller as a part
The hotel room charge includes breakfast. (호텔방값은 조식을 포함한다.)

3. benefit (득을 보다) to be helped by something
I have benefited greatly from her wisdom. (나는 그녀의 지혜에 득을 봤다.)

4. warn (경고하다) to give notice to a person of danger
I warn you that it is dangerous. (경고하는데 그건 위험하다.)

5. criticize (비판하다) to censure or find fault with
You were right to criticize him. (당신이 그를 비판한 것은 옳았다.)

6. hostility (적대감) opposition or resistance to an idea, plan
They had hostility to the man. (그들은 그 남자에게 적대감이 있다.)

7. respond (응답하다) to reply or answer in words
Do I have to respond now? (지금 답을 해야 하나요?)

8. promote (촉진하다) to help further the growth
My goal is to promote foreign investment. (나의 목표는 해외투자를 촉진하는 것이다.)

9. cooperation (협조) working together with someone
Thanks for your cooperation and support. (협조와 도움에 감사 드립니다.)

10. expand (확대하다) to increase in size, number, or importance
She wants to expand her business. (그녀는 사업을 확대하고 싶다.)

B. 빈칸에 알맞은 표현을 넣으시오.

began with,	no longer,	had a big impact on,	getting tired of,	make efforts
(~로 시작하다)	(더 이상~ 아닌)	(영향을 주다)	(지겨워하게 되다)	(노력하다)

1. Some foreigners are ( ) seeing the same old things over and over again.
2. K- pop music groups and singers have ( ) their fans.
3. It is ( ) surprising to see large groups of fans.
4. Korea should ( ) to promote itself to improve its image everywhere.
5. The Korean Wave first ( ) a few Korean TV programs and films.

LET'S READ IT TOGETHER

The Korean Wave: Past, Present and Future

1 "Hallyu" or Korean Wave, is a phrase first coined by a Chinese journalist in the mid-1990s. Since then, Korean entertainment has become a global sensation. The Korean Wave first began with a few Korean TV programs and films aired in several Asian countries, including Japan, China, and Thailand. Most recently, the popularity of the Korean Wave has grown to include K-pop music and online games, and has spread into Europe and the Americas. It is no longer surprising to see large groups of fans eagerly waiting for their favorite Korean stars to appear at international airports.

2 In many ways, the Korean Wave has greatly benefitted Korea economically and culturally. For example, every year millions of tourists from all over the world come to Korea to visit film locations of their favorite shows or movies. In 2011 for instance, 400,000 tourists visited Namiseom, where "Winter Sonata" was filmed. In addition, K- pop music groups and singers have had a big impact on their fans, especially on their tastes in food, fashion, make-up trends, and even plastic surgery. As a result, Korean products have become "must-have" items for many people around the world. Furthermore, some foreigners want to know more about Korean culture. In fact, many people are showing their interest in learning Korean as a foreign language. The number of students who learn Korean continues to increase.

Quick Comprehension Questions

1. Who coined the phrase, "Hallyu"?
2. Why is Namiseom popular among foreign tourists?
3. What impact have K-pop music groups and singers had on their fans?

vocabulary

phrase(어구) coin(말을 만들다) air(방송하다) appear(나타나다)
location(현장) film(영화를 찍다) taste(취향) make-up(화장)
trend(경향) plastic surgery(성형수술) must-have(반드시 가져야 할 것)

3 Despite this international popularity, there are those who warn that Korea will not be able to continue this successful ride on the Korean Wave in the future. According to a recent survey, many people see that the current high interest in Korean culture will not last long. In fact, some foreigners are getting tired of seeing the same things over and over again. For example, some point out that various K-pop singers wear the similar types of clothing, do similar dance moves, and use similar sounding lyrics. Korean soap operas are also criticized for focusing on the repeated themes of love triangles and revenge. In a few countries like Japan, the Korean Wave has even created hostility. Some Japanese are protesting against TV stations broadcasting Korean shows. Experts believe it is time for a change.

4 Fortunately, Korea is responding to these challenges. Some Korean entertainment industries have started to use Internet technologies and social media, such as YouTube and social network sites (SNSs) as new drive engines for the Korean Wave. Also, the Korean government is taking measures to boost the Korean wave by holding a variety of cultural events and pursuing global scale cooperation with other countries. Although it is not an easy task to continue and expand the Korean Wave, Korea should keep making efforts to promote itself to improve its image everywhere.

Quick Comprehension Questions

1. What are the repeated themes of Korean soap operas?
2. Where are people protesting against TV stations broadcasting Korean shows?
3. What have some Korean creative industries started to use?

vocabulary

popularity(인기) survey(설문조사) over and over again(계속 반복해서)
point out(지적하다) lyric(가사) focus on ~ (~에 초점을 맞추다) theme(주제)
love triangles(삼각관계) revenge(복수) TV station(TV 방송국)
broadcast(방영하다) expert(전문가) drive engine(동력)
take measures(조치를 취하다) pursue(추구하다)

READING COMPREHENSION

A. Understanding the Main Idea: 본문의 요지로 알맞은 것을 고르시오.

1. Ways to continue and expand the Korea Wave
2. Hostility toward the Korea Wave
3. Bright and dark sides of the Korea Wave
4. International popularity of the Korea Wave

B. Text Organization

각각의 주제에 해당하는 내용을 완성하시오.

1 Benefits of Korea Wave

A. Economical Benefits
  i. Millions of tourists come to Korea to ________________ ____.
  ii. Korean products have become ________________.
B. Cultural Benefits
  i. Many people getting interested in ________________.

2 Challenges to Korea Wave

A. Many people see that the popularity of the Korean Wave will ________________________________.
B. The fans are ______________ of K-pop music and soap operas.
  i. K-pop singers: ________________ types of clothing, dancing moves, and lyrics.
  ii. TV dramas: repeated themes of _______ and _______.
C. Hostility against the Korean Wave
  i. Japanese protest against ____________________.

3 Responses to Challenges

A. Korean entertainment industries
  i. Using the Internet and social media as ______________.
B. the Korean government
  i. Holding a variety of ________________________.
  ii. Pursuing ____________________ with other countries.

C. Understanding Details:
아래의 문장이 본문의 내용과 맞으면 T, 틀리면 F를 선택하시오.

	True	False
1. It is common that a lot of fans wait for their favorite Korean stars at the airports.		
2. The Korean Wave helped Korean products sell well abroad.		
3. No one believes the current high interest in Korean culture will continue long.		
4. Some foreigners are tired of listening to new K-pop music.		
5. Some Korean creative industries have started to hold a variety of cultural events.		
6. K- pop singers have benefitted their fans economically.		

D. Reading Strategy

뜻을 모르는 단어 의미 추론 (Dealing with Unfamiliar Words)

영어로 글을 읽을 때 뜻을 모르는 단어에 맛 부닥치는 경우가 많다. 그럴 때 마다 **사전을 찾기 보다는 이미 아는 단어를 통해 그 단어가 들어 있는 문장의 앞 뒤 전후 맥락을 개략적으로 이해하면서 그 단어의 의미를 추론해 보는 것이 효과적이다.** 예를 들어 다음 글에서 밑줄 친 hostility라는 단어의 뜻을 모른다고 할 때,

In a few countries like Japan, the Korean Wave has even created **hostility**. Some Japanese are protesting against TV stations broadcasting Korean shows.

우선 이 글의 전반적인 내용을 이해하자. 즉 한류가 일본 포함 몇 나라에서 hostility 낳고 있고 두 번째 문장에서는 일본에서 한국 드라마 방영에 반대하는 데모가 벌어지고 있다고 한다. 이로부터 hostility는 뭔가 안 좋은 의미의 단어라고 추측할 수 있다. 그러면 이제 hostility가 뭐길래 사람들이 데모를 하게 만들까 생각해 보라. 사람들이 데모를 하는 것은 어떤 대상에 대해 반발하는 마음이 있을 때이다. 그렇다면 한류가 일본인들을 반발하는 마음이 들게 만들었다고 추론할 수 있을 것이다. 이 정도만 해도 글을 이해하는 데는 충분하지만, 단어의 정확한 뜻을 알고 싶으면 사전을 찾아 확인해 보면 된다.

위의 설명을 기반으로 아래 글을 읽으며 밑줄 친 단어들의 뜻을 추론해 보시오.

In fact, some foreigners are getting tired of seeing the same things over and over again. For example, some **complain** that various K-pop singers wear the similar types of clothing, do similar dance moves, and use similar sounding lyrics. Korean soap operas are also **criticized** for focusing on the repeated themes of love triangles and revenge.

VOCABULARY REVIEW

A. 빈칸에 알맞은 단어를 넣으시오.

expand	cooperation	criticize	warn	benefit	spread	respond	includes

1. Bad news ____________ faster than good news.
2. The price ____________ : breakfast, pool and lounge.
3. They are working together to ____________ the entire company.
4. The authors ____________ that the road will cause an environmental disaster.
5. I'm a Christian, and I don't ____________ other religions.
6. ____________ with others is very important for success in business.
7. She read a lot of books to ____________ her knowledge of philosophy.
8. The U.S. wait and see how North Korea ______________ before they make their next move.

B. Word Power

Must + verb ⇨ Noun

영어에서는 'must-have'와 같이 두 개 이상의 단어를 결합하여 새로운 단어를 만들어 내는 것이 흔하다. 이를 복합어(compound word)라고 하는 데 이런 방식으로 단어를 만들어 쓰면 제한된 수의 단어로 원하는 표현을 거의 무한정 만들 수 있다는 장점이 있다.

Must + see ⇨ must-see (꼭 보아야 할 것 / 볼 만한 것)
Must + read ⇨ must-read (꼭 읽어야 할 것 / 읽을 만한 것)
Must + go ⇨ must-go (꼭 가봐야 할 곳 / 가 볼 만한 곳)
Must + try ⇨ must-try (꼭 해봐야 할 것 / 해 볼 만한 것)

1. *Titanic* is definitely a **must-see** movie.
   (타이태닉은 반드시 봐야 할 영화다)
2. The biography of Lincoln is in the **must-read** list.
   (링컨의 전기문은 필독 목록에 있다)
3. There are so many **must-go** places in New York.
   (뉴욕에는 반드시 가야 할 장소가 많다)
4. Do you know any **must-try** restaurants in Busan?
   (부산에서 꼭 가볼 만한 식당을 아니?)

GRAMMAR FOCUS

장소를 표현하는 전치사

in 과 at 은 장소를 표시하기도 한다. in은 주로 대륙이나 나라와 같이 큰 지역이나 '~안에서'라는 뜻으로 사용된다. at은 어떤 장소, 특히 상호가 있는 장소에서 하는 활동을 표현할 때 주로 사용한다. 관사 없이 특정 장소와 함께 사용될 때 그 곳에서 하는 활동을 나타내기도 한다.

The Day of the Dead is actually a celebration **in** Mexico.
In a few countries like Japan, the Korean Wave has created hostility.
The girls are waiting for their favorite stars **at** international airports.
People spend the whole night **at** the grave.

IN	AT
■ 대륙, 나라, 도시 **In** Europe, **in** China, **in** Seoul Psy is very popular **in** America.	■ 어떤 장소, 특히 상호가 있는 장소 We went shopping **at** the mall. Let's have lunch **at** McDonald's.
■ 어떤 장소 안이라는 뜻 **in** the store, **in** the box, **in** the car I'll wait **in** the store. Put the books **in** the box.	■ 관사 없이 바로 장소 **at** work : 일하는 중, 일하면서 **at** home: 집에(서) **at** school: 학교에(서)

Be careful: at과 in의 차이에 주의할 것
Let's meet **at** McDonald's. : 맥도날드에서(그 지점) 만나자.
Let's meet **in** McDonald's. : 맥도날드 **안에서** 만나자.

A. 알맞은 전치사를 넣어 문장을 완성하시오.

1. Some people listen to music (at/in) work.
2. My brother grew up (at/in) Busan.
3. You should stay (at/in) home tonight.
4. Some children like to read books (at/in) the car.

B. 다음 글을 읽고 틀린 부분을 찾아 맞게 고치시오.

Yesterday, we went shopping in K-mart. On our way to there, my son listened to music at the car. There were a lot of people at the store. We bought a Teddy Bear at the toy section and then went to a Thai restaurant. We had to wait a long time to be served because there were so many people at the restaurant. My wife and son were so tired they fell asleep at the car.

LET'S TALK ABOUT IT

A. 다음 대화를 듣고 연습해 봅시다

Sujin: I'm going to go to a Psy concert this Saturday.
Chris: I didn't know you were a fan of Psy.
Sujin: Oh, I'm not just a fan, I'm a member of his fan club!
Chris: **No way!**
Sujin: **Hard to believe, isn't it?**
Chris: **Since when were you** a member?
Sujin: I joined when he released his first album.

B. 의사소통 기능:

1. **No way!** (말도 안돼. 어림없어)는 어떤 사실에 대해 믿겨지지 않는 다는 뜻을 표현할 때 사용한다.

   A: We can finish the homework by five o'clock. (우리 다섯 시까지 숙제 마칠 수 있어.)
   B: **No way!** (어림없어!)

2. **Hard to believe, isn't it?** (믿기 어렵지, 그렇지?)는 It's hard to believe, isn't it?의 준말이다. 구어체에서는 이렇게 문장의 일부를 생략해서 사용하는 경우가 많다.

3. **Since when were you a member?** (너 언제부터 회원이었어?)의 문법적으로는 옳지 않은 문장이다. Since~(~이래로) 사용했으므로 현재 완료형을 사용해야 한다. **Since when have you been a member?** 이 문법적으로 정확한 표현이다. 하지만 구어체에서는 이렇게 문법적으로 옳지 않은 문장을 습관적으로 쓰는 경우가 있다.

C. 말해보기: 아래 빈칸에 알맞은 표현을 넣으시오.

1. A: I got straight As this semester. (이번 학기에 전과목 A받았어.)
   B: ____________________. (말도 안돼.)
   A: ____________________, isn't it? (믿기 어렵지, 그렇지?)

2. A: __________________ a HYCU student? (너 언제부터 한양 사이버대 학생이었니?)
   B: I entered HYCU three years ago. (3년 전에 입학했어.)

COMMON ERRORS IN ENGLISH

Dramas vs. Soap operas

Sujin: Did you know Korean entertainment is very popular in China.
Karen: Films or television?
Sujin: Well, both, but especially Korean **dramas**.
Karen: Korean dramas? You mean Korean **soap operas**?
Sujin: Ohh.. You're right, Korean soap operas.

1. 한국에서는 TV 연속극을 drama라고 부르지만 원래 서구에서 drama란 '텔레비전에 나오는 통속극' 말고도 방송, 연극, 영화, 기타 장르를 아우르는 용어이다. 따라서 영어로 drama라고 말하면 외국인들은 주로 연극이나 영화라고 생각하는 경우가 많다.

2. drama라는 말 대신에, 특히 미국에서는 **Soap opera** 또는 **TV show**라고 부른다. 이는 보통 오전 11시에서 오후 2시 사이에 TV 연속극을 가리키는 데, 우리나라의 드라마와 내용과 구성이 비슷하다. 이들 연속극의 주 시청자들이 주부들이었는데 이들을 주 고객으로 하는 비누나 세제 회사들이 제작자나 광고주였던 까닭에 **Soap opera**라는 말이 생겨났다고 한다. 줄여서 **soaps**라고도 부른다.

3. 참고로 소위 미드라고 부르는 Friends, Law and city등은 **TV series**라고 부릅니다. 그리고 정 drama라는 말을 쓰고 싶으면 **TV drama**라고 하면 된다. 한류의 영향으로 우리가 계속 drama라고 말하다 보면 drama가 우리가 뜻하는 단어가 될 날이 올 수도 있다. 언어는 고정불변이 아니라 늘 변화하는 것이다.

Answer Key

Lesson 1 YOU ARE WHAT YOU EAT

WARM UP

B. 1. She likes to eat chocolate, peanut butter and hamburgers.
   2. She eats three meals a day.
   3. She needs to watch her eating habits first.

VOCABULARY PREVIEW

A. 1. cut down on / 2. such as / 3. start off / 4. when it comes to / 5. take time

LET'S READ IT TOGETHER

Quick Comprehension Questions

1. They are carbohydrates, fats, proteins, minerals, and vitamins.
2. You can find them in nuts, seeds, olives and fish such as salmon.
3. Vegetables and fruits are rich in minerals and vitamins.

Quick Comprehension Questions

1. Vegetables, fruits, whole grains and healthy fats are necessary for eating smart.
2. You need to cut down on portion size, take time to chew your food, and eat breakfast.
3. It makes your energy go through quick ups and downs.

READING COMPREHENSION

A. 3
B. 1. e / 2. b / 3. d / 4. f / 5. c / 6. a
C. 1. F / 2. F / 3. T / 4. T / 5. F / 6. F
D. 1

VOCABULARY REVIEW

A. 1.reduce / 2.consume / 3.prevent/ 4.maintain/ 5.chew / 6.contain / 7.tip / 8.essential

GRAMMAR FOCUS

A. 1. Be quiet in the classroom. / 2. do not eat saturated fat.
B. To keep your body healthy, a healthy diet is very important. First, <u>be</u> careful when you choose food. Second, <u>learn</u> about essential nutrients before grocery shopping. Third, <u>limit</u> your sugar and salt intake. Also, <u>do not eat</u> food that contains unhealthy fat. When you have meals, <u>chew</u> your food and <u>stop</u> eating before you feel full.

LET'S TALK ABOUT IT

C. 1. That sounds good! 2. that's terrific.

Lesson 2 LET'S WORK OUT

WARM UP

B. 1. He is going to eat healthy food.
   2. Because he is really busy.
   3. Stretching is a good exercise to do at home.

VOCABULARY PREVIEW

A. 1. based on / 2. In general / 3. in addition to / 4. plenty of / 5. instead of

LET'S READ IT TOGETHER

Quick Comprehension Questions

1. We should get 30–60 minutes of physical activity everyday.
2. It includes aerobic exercise, strength training, and flexibility training.
3. Pull–ups and push–ups are good for the shoulders and chest.

Quick Comprehension Questions

1. Stretching, gymnastics, and yoga are good for flexibility training.
2. Exercise can help prevent diseases and reduce stress.
3. You need to consider cutting down on calories.

READING COMPREHENSION

A. 2
B. 1. d / 2. a / 3. b / 4. f / 5. c / 6. e
C. 1. F / 2. F / 3. T / 4. T / 5. F / 6. T
D. Paragraph 1: We need to exercise to stay healthy.
   Paragraph 2–4: A well–balanced exercise workout includes aerobic exercise, strength training, and flexibility training.
   Paragraph 5: Choose the right exercise for you.

VOCABULARY REVIEW

1. deliver / 2. physical / 3. flexibility / 4. prefer / 5.involve / 6. injury / 7. strengthen / 8. burn

GRAMMAR FOCUS

A. 1. less handsome 또는 more handsome / 2. faster / 3. prettier / 4. hotter
B. Chris and his younger brother John exercise every morning together. Usually, Chris runs longer than his brother because he is bigger than him. But John can do more sit–ups and pull–ups than his brother because he is leaner than Chris.)

LET'S TALK ABOUT IT

C. 1. would like to   2. hope

Answer Key

Lesson 3 I DON'T KNOW WHAT TO WEAR

WARM UP

B.

1. She likes to wear anything that makes her look unique.
2. Yes, she has a lot of clothes in her closet.
3. She needs to get rid of clothing that is out of date.

VOCABULARY PREVIEW

A. 1. out of date / 2. looks good on / 3. according to / 4. find out / 5. Get rid of

LET'S READ IT TOGETHER

Quick Comprehension Questions

1. Because they say a lot about who we are and what we are feeling, to others around us.
2. You need to know your body type and what kinds of clothing are well fitted for you.
3. It is checking if you have clothing that you bought 10 or more years ago.

Quick Comprehension Questions

1. Vertical stripes make you look taller.
2. Because it plays a big part in your image.
3. It is "dress to impress."

READING COMPREHENSION

A. 2

B. 1. c / 2. b/ 3. d/ 4. a

C. 1. T/ 2. F / 3. T / 4. T / 5. F / 6. T

D. 1. d / 2. a / 3. c/ 4. e / 5 b

VOCABULARY REVIEW

A. 1. favorite / 2. stylish / 3. appears / 4. fit / 5. opportunities / 6. match / 7. organize / 8. current

GRAMMAR FOCUS

A. 1. who 또는 that / 2. which 또는 that / 3. which 또는 that / 4. who 또는 that

B. If you are a person who wants to dress with style, you need to know your body type. To follow current fashion trends, you need to get rid of clothing that (또는 which) is out of date. After that, try to find colors that (또는which) look good on you.)

LET'S TALK ABOUT IT

C. 1. How about 2. Let's

Lesson 4 AN AMERICAN WHO WAS MORE KOREAN THAN KOREANS

WARM UP

B. 1. F/ 2. T/ 3. T

VOCABULARY PREVIEW

B. 1. is full of / 2. fell in love with / 3. happened to / 4. became interested in / 5. died of

Let's read it together

Quick Comprehension Questions

1. It is in Taean, South Chungcheong Province.
2. He went hiking in the mountains.
3. It was in 1952.

Quick Comprehension Questions

1. It was in 2000.
2. It is Min Byung-gal.
3. Because he wanted to preserve and protect it

READING COMPREHENSION

A. 3
B. 1945: e / 1952: d / 1962: a / 1979: c, f / 2000: b
C. 1. F / 2. F / 3. F / 4. F / 5. F / 6. T
D. 5 / 6 / 2 / 4 / 3

VOCABULARY REVIEW

1. valuable / 2. environment / 3. rare / 4. raises / 5. awarded / 6. preserve / 7. anxious / 8. established

GRAMMAR FOCUS

(fell) / (went) / (became) / (bought) / (said) / (got) / (ate)
A. 1. became / 2. fell / 3. built / 4. got
B. Yesterday, I went to Lotte Department with my sister. At the clothing section, my sister bought a skirt, and then we saw a new Spielberg movie, which was very fun. After the movie, we went to Starbucks. We drank coffee and ate some sandwiches. On our way home, my sister said, "it was a great day."

LET'S TALK ABOUT IT

B. 2. 1) Nothing special (or much) 2) It was (great / wonderful / awesome)

Answer Key

Lesson 5 A CHEROKEE WOMAN WHO MADE A DIFFERENCE

WARM UP

B. 1. F / 2. T / 3. F

VOCABULARY PREVIEW

B. 1. played an important role in / 2. participated in / 3. ran for / 4. suffered from / 5. made fun of

LET'S READ IT TOGETHER

Quick Comprehension Questions

1. She was born in a small town, Tahlequah, Oklahoma.
2. She moved there when she was 12.
3. They did it to protest against unfair treatment of the Native American people.

Quick Comprehension Questions

1. She was seriously injured in a car accident.
2. It was in 1985.
3. Because she was a woman.

READING COMPREHENSION

A. 2

B. para 1. d / para 2. g / para 3. b / para 4. f / para 5. c / para 6. a / para 7. e

C. 1. F / 2. F / 3. F / 4. T / 5. T / 6. F

D. 1. She worked hard to help the Cherokee people improve their living conditions.
2. because she decided to live for the Cherokee people.

VOCABULARY REVIEW

1. population / 2. protesting / 3. progress / 4. overcome / 5. injured / 6. remember / 7. mourns / 8. government

GRAMMAR FOCUS

A. 1. at / 2. in / 3. On / 4. in

B. Wilma Mankiller, the first female chief of the Cherokee Nation, passed away on April 6, 2010. She became principal chief in 1987 and led the Cherokee Nation for 10 years. On Tuesday, President Obama expressed his sadness about her death. Funeral Services will be held at the Indian Ministry, 3045 Park Avenue South, Minneapolis, at 10:00 a.m. on Wednesday, April 14.

LET'S TALK ABOUT IT.

C. 1. you can recommend?
2. A: Have you read / B: I've heard of it

Lesson 6 VOICES OF HYCU STUDENTS

WARM UP

B. 1. F / 2. T / 3. T

VOCABULARY PREVIEW

1. look up / 2. turn on / 3. succeeded in / 4. in the end / 5. am busy

LET'S READ IT TOGETHER

Quick Comprehension Questions

1. She does housework.
2. It took him 3 and a half years.

Quick Comprehension Questions

1. He communicates with pilots to help guide air traffic.
2. Because she can see that her English is getting better.

READING COMPREHENSION

A. 1
B. Lee (c, 1) / Kim (a, 3) / Jung (b,4) / Yoon (d,2)
C. 1. F / 2. T / 3. T / 4. F / 5. F / 6. F
D. 1. 2 / 2. 1

VOCABULARY REVIEW

A. 1. motivate / 2. leave / 3. wonder / 4. frustrating / 5.communicate / 6. ideal / 7. earn / 8. determined

GRAMMAR FOCUS

A. 1. usually plays / 2. never go / 3. am always / 4. Sometimes, Mike.. or Mike couldn't sometimes
B. Kyung-eun is always very busy. She usually gets up at 6 in the morning. During the daytime, she teaches English at a private language institute. At night, she takes online lectures. She sometimes feels very tired, but she never goes to bed before midnight.

LET'S TALK ABOUT IT

C. 1. you decided what to do / 2. your plans work out

Answer Key

Lesson 8 WRITING TIPS: PUNCTUATION

I. Capitalization

B. 1. My birthday is next Friday.
   2. Her favorite actor is Tom Cruise.
   3. Some people don't know Korea is located in Asia.
   4. Americans celebrate Martin Luther King Day in the winter.

C. My name is Carl Miller. I was born in Pennsylvania, U.S.A. in 1921. I served the U.S. Navy during World War II and then came to Korea in 1945. From early 1970s, I started to build a garden in Chollipo and I finally established the Chollipo Arboretum. It was awarded the "Arboretum Distinguished for Merit", the first time in Asia.

II. Comma (,) with Items in a Series

B. 1. Fish, poultry, and eggs are important sources of protein.
   2. It should contain essential nutrients such as carbohydrates, fats, protein, minerals, and vitamins.
   3. My sister always eats fruits and vegetables for lunch.
   4. Karen, Andy, and Paul like to eat Ramen.
   5. Nuts and seeds are good sources of healthy fats.

C. My brother and I have different tastes of foods. For example, I like to have eggs, bacon, and coffee for breakfast. But my brother eats toast, fruits, and milk in the morning. So my mother is very busy preparing them every morning. Usually Mom goes grocery shopping to buy milk, orange juice, coffee, bacon, and eggs. But I changed my mind to eat different kinds of food. Yesterday, I went grocery shopping. I bought bread, cereal, apples, bananas, and tomatoes. My brother was very glad because he could eat apples and bananas.

III. Comma (,) with Introductory Phrases and Clauses

B. 1. Before Victor was found, he apparently lived his entire childhood alone in the woods.
   2. Occasionally, Victor spoke a few words, but that was all.
   3. For one thing, Korean parents seem to wish that at least their children's pronunciation will be very good.
   4. According to some studies, motivation, anxiety, and time commitment are equally important.
   5. When I entered the first grade in elementary school, I began learning how to read.

C. Around the time I reached puberty, I began learning English. When I was a student in elementary school, English was not an official subject to study. At the age of 14, I started learning the English alphabet. Because I wanted to understand what American people said on TV, I studied English very hard. I also enjoyed learning English and spent a lot of time in speaking and listening to English. Finally, when I was a senior at university, I was chosen to study abroad in the U.S.

Lesson 9 LANGUAGE LEARNING FACTORS

WARM UP

B. 1. T / 2. F / 3. T

VOCABULARY PREVIEW

B. 1. in the first place / 2. by herself / 3. ended up / 4. make our best efforts / 5. go on

LET'S READ IT TOGETHER

Quick Comprehension Questions

1. It is about love.
2. They learn to sing in their early years.

Quick Comprehension Questions

1. Younger (before puberty) is better.
2. Motivation and time commitment

READING COMPREHENSION

A. 2

B. 2 / 1 / 4 / 3 / 5

C. 1. F / 2. F / 3. F / 4. F / 5. T / 6. T

D. 1. Topic sentence / 2. Supporting details / 3. Supporting details / 4. Supporting details / 5. Supporting details / 6. Supporting details

VOCABULARY REVIEW

A. 1. dark / 2. age / 3. expert / 4. critical / 5. research / 6. apply / 7. factors / 8. lyrics

GRAMMAR FOCUS

A. 1. was built / 2. is spoken / 3. were raised / 4. was discovered

B. Genie was found in 1970 in California. When she was found, she was 13 years old but could not speak except for short phrases. The reason was because she was tied to a potty chair until she became 13 years old and was left alone in a dark room. Almost no one, not even her parents, met or talked with her often.

LET'S TALK ABOUT IT

1. We should get together again sometime. / Let's get together again sometime. / Why don't we get together again sometime?
2. Coffee's on me! / Coffee's my treat!

Answer Key

Lesson 10 BODY LANGUAGE DIFFERS ACROSS CULTURES

WARM UP

B. 1. T / 2. T / 3. F

VOCABULARY PREVIEW

B. 1. It seems that / 2. call over / 3. In parts of / 4. go to / 5. More than

LET'S READ IT TOGETHER

Quick Comprehension Questions

1. Silent language
2. No
3. More than half of what we communicate

Quick Comprehension Questions

1. Comfort zone
2. Body language can be more important than speaking.

READING COMPREHENSION

A. 4
B. 3 / 2 / 5 / 4 / 1
C. 1. T / 2. T / 3. F / 4. F / 5. T / 6. T
D. 1. Summary / 2. Recommendation / 3. Prediction

VOCABULARY REVIEW

A. 1. convey / 2. signal / 3. opposite / 4. way / 5. rude / 6. including / 7. abroad / 8. mistaken

GRAMMAR FOCUS

A. 1. the closest / 2. the loudest / 3. the most interesting / 4. the most personal
B. When we talk about cultural differences, body language is perhaps <u>the most</u> interesting topic to discuss. One of <u>the most</u> obvious differences can be seen in people's hand gestures. In Korea, for the "come here" gesture, the palm is downward and the fingers are moved back and forth. However, in the U.S., they show the "come here" gesture in the opposite way. Their palm is upward, and they move their fingers back and forth.

LET'S TALK ABOUT IT

1. I think
2. I don't think

Lesson 11 MEN AND WOMEN COMMUNICATE DIFFERENTLY

WARM UP

B. 1. F / 2. F / 3. T

VOCABULARY PREVIEW

B. 1. are described as / 2. In contrast / 3. compete with / 4. learn about / 5. For instance

LET'S READ IT TOGETHER

Quick Comprehension Questions

1. John Gray
2. A professor at an American university
3. Girls

Quick Comprehension Questions

1. Referring to men or women
2. As either a single or married man

READING COMPREHENSION

A. 4
B. 1 / 3 / 2 / 4 / 5
C. 1. F / 2. F / 3. T / 4. T / 5. T / 6. F
D. 1. In contrast / 2. Similarly / but

VOCABULARY REVIEW

A. 1. cooperative / 2. describe / 3. fascinating / 4. behave / 5. annoyed / 6. rapport / 7. identify / 8. instantly

GRAMMAR FOCUS

A. 1. why Jane is smiling / 2. who that man is / 3. why you cried / 4. how Tom got
B. I met an old friend last Sunday. We hadn't seen each other for a long time so we had a lot of questions for each other. He asked how I was doing and where I was living. He also asked what my job was. For me, I asked him if he was married. He said he was. I can't believe he's married and has children. In my eyes, he is still a little kid who I played with in my childhood.

LET'S TALK ABOUT IT

1. It seems like / It seems that / It appears that / I get the impression that
2. It seems like / It seems that / It appears that / I get the impression that

Answer Key

Lesson 12 A FOREIGNER'S EXPERIENCES IN KOREA

WARM UP

B. 1. F / 2. F / 3. F

VOCABULARY PREVIEW

B. 1. am used to / 2. as soon as / 3. burst into laughter / 4. for free / 5. are different from

LET'S READ IT TOGETHER

Quick Comprehension Questions

1. She uses her blog.
2. Because the walls were made of mud and fairly think.
3. Two nights.

Quick Comprehension Questions

1. They are similar to those in her home country.
2. A lot of the stalls selling fresh fish, vegetables, rice cakes, kimbap and so on..
3. Because she tried to do a Korean traditional bow on the floor but she fell over.

READING COMPREHENSION

A. 2

B. 1. heated via Ondol / more air flow/ fresh / mud / fairly thick / hear any noise /
2. similar / a lot of different sections / delicious / cheap / helpings for free / beautiful / look like an angel

C. 1. F / 2. F / 3. T / 4. T / 5. F / 6. F

D. 1. F / 2.F / 3. O / 4. F / 5. O / 6. F

VOCABULARY REVIEW

A. 1. worried / 2. allow / 3. noise / 4. faces / 5. admits / 6. assume / 7. additional / 8. stroll

B. 1. to / 2. fall / 3. without / 4. get / 5. well (or soundly)

GRAMMAR FOCUS

A. 1. surprising, surprised / 2. boring, bored / 3. interested, interesting / 4. excited, exciting / 5. tired, tiring

B. Chris has an <u>amazing</u> personality. He knows how to cheer people up. For example, whenever the meeting is <u>boring</u>, he tells <u>interesting</u> stories that get everyone involved in the discussion again. We are all very <u>excited</u> to work with Chris.

LET'S TALK ABOUT IT

C. 1. A: what should I see there? B: should definitely / 2. should not miss

Lesson 13 HOLIDAYS AROUND THE WORLD

WARM UP

B. 1. F / 2. T / 3. T

VOCABULARY PREVIEW

B. 1. get together / 2. light up / 3. gave out / 4. At first glance / 5. dress up in

LET'S READ IT TOGETHER

Quick Comprehension Questions

1. It lasts for three days.
2. To remember and honor their ancestors
3. They spend the whole night at the grave.

Quick Comprehension Questions

1. They believe this will give them good lick for the New Year.
2. It is during the last two days and the first two days of the Hindu lunar month.
3. She is the goddess of wealth.

READING COMPREHENSION

A. 3

B. the Day of the Dead: Mexico / Oct. 31 to Nov. 2 / their ancestors / relatives / flowers, earth and candles / their ancestor's favorite foods / masks and costumes

the Festival of Lights : India / last two days and first two days of Hindu lunar month / the start of New Year / clean / decorate / good luck / anger, hate and jealousy

C. 1. T / 2. F / 3. F / 4. F / 5. F / 6. F

D. American holiday / New Orleans, Louisiana / the 1700s / several weeks / the early part of the year / over 60 / things such as necklaces, false money / clothes

VOCABULARY REVIEW

A. 1. ancestors / 2. decorate / 3. last / 4. custom / 5. attend / 6. blessed / 7. pray / 8. remove

GRAMMAR FOCUS

A. 1. speaks / 2. live / 3. are / 4. enjoys / 5. love

B. On the last day of the year, the people of Spain get together with their friends and wait until midnight. Everyone has twelve grapes ready to eat at midnight. When the clock starts to chime, people put a grape in their mouth, one grape for each stroke of the clock. When the chiming ends, all the people have mouthful of grapes.

LET'S TALK ABOUT IT

C. 1. Is it true / 2. Don't take it so seriously

Answer Key

Lesson 14 THE KOREAN WAVE: PAST, PRESENT AND FUTURE

WARM UP

B. 1. T / 2. F / 3. F

VOCABULARY PREVIEW

B. 1. getting tired of / 2. had a big impact on / 3. no longer / 4. make efforts / 5. began with

LET'S READ IT TOGETHER

Quick Comprehension Questions

1. A Chinese journalist did.
2. Because "Winter Sonata" was filmed there.
3. On their tastes in food, fashion, make-up trends, and even plastic surgery.

Quick Comprehension Questions

1. Love triangles and revenge.
2. In Japan.
3. They have started to use Internet technologies and social media, such as YouTube and social network sites (SMSs).

READING COMPREHENSION

A. 3

B. 1. A. i. visit film location of the favorite shows. / ii. "must-have" items / B. i. learning Korean as a foreign language / 2. A. not last long / b. getting tired / i. similar / ii. love triangles, revenge / C. i. TV stations broadcasting Korean shows. / 3. A. i. new drive engines / B. i. cultural events / ii. global scale cooperation

C. 1. T / 2.T / 3.F / 4.F / 5.F / 6.F

D. complain : 불쾌한, criticized: 비판하다.

VOCABULARY REVIEW

A. 1. spread / 2. includes / 3. benefit / 4. warn / 5. criticize / 6. Cooperation / 7. expend / 8. respond

GRAMMAR FOCUS

A. 1. at / 2. in / 3. at / 4. in

B. Yesterday, we went shopping <u>at</u> K-mart. On our way to there, my son listened to music <u>in</u> the car. There were a lot of people <u>in</u> the store. We bought a Teddy Bear at the toy section and then went to a Thai restaurant. We had to wait a long time to be served because there were so many people <u>in</u> the restaurant. My wife and son were so tired they fell asleep <u>in</u> the car.

LET'S TALK ABOUT IT

C. 1. B: No way. A: Hard to believe / 2. Since when were you

Translation

Lesson 1 YOU ARE WHAT YOU EAT

1 "먹는 것이 당신을 말해주고 있다" 라는 속담을 들어 본 적이 있는가? 이것은 우리가 먹는 것이 우리의 건강에 영향을 준다는 뜻이다. 음식의 선택과 식습관에 관해서 고려해야 할 몇 가지 사항들이 있다.

2 건강하고 균형 있는 음식은 건강을 유지하고 증진 시키는 것을 도와준다. 그래서 식사(meal)는 탄수화물, 지방, 단백질, 미네랄과 비타민과 같은 필수 영양소를 포함하고 있어야 한다. 탄수화물은 신체 에너지의 주된 원천이고 쌀, 빵, 감자 등에 있다. 몸을 강하게 유지하고 질병을 예방하기 위해서 우리는 건강에 좋은 지방이 또한 필요하다. 우리 몸이 필요로 하는 건강한 지방의 좋은 원천으로는 견과류, 씨, 올리브와 연어와 같은 생선이 있다.

3 단백질은 근육과 신체기관을 만들고 유지한다. 고기, 생선, 가금류와 계란은 단백질의 중요한 원천이다. 생선은 심장병의 위험을 줄일 수 있다. 그러나 붉은색 고기와 버터는 질병의 위험을 증가 시킬 수 있는 포화 지방을 많이 포함하고 있다. 미네랄과 비타민도 또한 우리 몸에 필수적이다. 예를 들면, 채소와 과일은 미네랄과 비타민이 많은데 이것들은 암이나 고혈압과 같은 질병으로부터 우리를 보호해 준다.

4 식습관은 올바르고 건강에 좋은 음식을 선택하는 것만큼 중요하다. 지혜롭게 먹는 몇 가지 조언들이 여기에 있다. 첫째, 필수 영양소들이 들어 있는 건강에 좋은 음식을 계획하는 것을 생각해 보라. 장을 보러 갈 때에는 채소, 과일, 통곡물과 좋은 단백질의 원천과 건강에 좋은 지방이 들어있는 것들을 선택하라. 둘째, 설탕과 소금의 섭취를 제한하라. 설탕은 에너지가 빨리 오르고 내리도록 한다. 소금 자체는 나쁘지 않다 하지만 대부분의 한국인들이 음식에서 너무 많은 소금을 섭취한다는 것을 기억하라.

5 셋째, 매끼 식사량을 줄이라. 외식을 할 때는 너무 많은 양을 주문하지 말라. 집에서는 작은 접시를 사용하는 것이 좋은 방법이다. 넷째, 식사하는 동안에는 음식을 천천히 씹고 배가 부르다고 느끼기 전에 식사를 마치라. 당신의 뇌가 당신의 몸에 충분한 음식을 먹었다고 알리는 데는 몇 분이 걸린다. 마지막으로 아침을 먹어라 왜냐하면 그것은 하루를 시작하는 가장 좋은 방법이기 때문이다. 하루 종일 적고 건강한 식사를 하는 것이 당신의 에너지를 올려주는 것임을 기억하라.

Translation

Lesson 2 LET'S WORK OUT

1 사회는 변하고 있고 더 많은 사람들이 어떤 종류이든 신체 활동이나 운동 하는 것을 원하지 않는다. 예를 들면 계단을 이용하는 대신에 사람들은 엘리베이터나 에스컬레이터를 사용하기를 더 좋아한다. 하지만 의사들은 건강하기 위해서는 매일 30-60분의 신체활동을 해야 한다고 말한다. 간단한 운동을 하는 것은 에너지 수준을 올리고 기분을 좋게 할 수 있다. 하지만 정말 건강하기 위해서는 올바른 형태의 운동을 선택하는 것이 더 중요하다.

2 균형 잡힌 운동(workout)에는 유산소 운동, 근력운동, 유연성 훈련이 있다. 유산소 운동은 심장을 뛰게 하는데 이것은 호흡을 많이 하고 몸 전체에 더 많은 산소를 전달하게 해서 심장을 튼튼하게 하는데 도움을 줄 수 있다. 유산소 운동의 예로는 뛰기, 자전거 타기, 수영과 에어로빅 댄스 등이 있다.

3 근력운동도 또한 도움이 되는데 이것은 오랜 기간 동안 해야 한다. 강한 근육을 만드는 것은 몸의 관절을 보호하고 부상을 막는데 도움을 준다. 서로 다른 부위의 근육을 강화 시키는 데는 다양한 운동들이 있다. 예를 들면 턱걸이와 팔굽혀 펴기는 어깨와 흉부에 좋다. 서서 무릎 구부리기와 다리 들어 올리기는 다리에 좋은 운동이다. 윗몸 일으키기와 누워서 윗몸 굽히기는 복부 근육에 좋은 운동이다. 같은 운동을 계속 반복하는 것이 좋은 방법이다.

4 유연성 훈련에는 근육을 유연하게 유지하는데 도움을 주는 구부리기와 스트레칭이 있는데 이것들은 부상을 막는데 도움을 줄 수 있다. 스트레칭, 체조와 요가 등의 활동이 유연성 훈련에 좋은 예이다. 운동 전과 중간 그리고 후에는 물을 많이 마시는 것이 중요하다.

5 초보자들에게는 일주일에 3일 하루에 약 20-30분 동안 하는 운동을 시작하는 것이 가장 좋다. 개인적으로 즐기고 효과가 있는 운동을 선택해야 한다. 헬스클럽에 가는 것도 건강 유지를 위한 또 하나의 좋은 방법이다. 그것은 혼자 운동하는 것을 좋아하지 않고 대신 다른 사람들과 같이 있는 것을 더 좋아하는 사람들에게 좋은 선택이 될 수 있다. 또한 칼로리를 태우기 위해서는 집안일을 하는 것뿐 아니라 걷기와 계단오르기 등도 매우 효과가 있다는 것을 기억하라.

6 그래서 일반적으로 운동은 질병을 예방하고 스트레스를 줄인다. 또한 운동은 더 좋게 보이고 기분을 좋게 한다. 체지방을 줄이고 근육량을 높이기 위해서는 운동과 함께 건강에 좋은 음식을 또한 같이 병행해야 한다. 그래서 누구든지 체중을 줄이고 싶다면 운동 하는 것 외에도 칼로리는 줄이는 것을 고려해야 한다. 무엇을 기다리고 있는가? 이제 운동을 하자!

1 당신은 옷 쇼핑하는 것을 좋아하는가? 옷은 편안함뿐 아니라 몸을 보호하는데도 중요하다. 당신은 멋진 옷을 입는 것을 좋아하는가 아니면 편안함이 더 중요한가? 우리가 입고 있는 것은 종종 우리 주위 사람들에게 우리가 누구 인지와 우리가 느끼고 있는 것에 대해 많은 것을 알려준다.

2 입을 옷을 준비할 때 당신이 편하고 최고로 보이게 하기 위해서 몇 가지 고려해야 할 것들이 있다. 첫째, 당신의 체형을 알고 어떤 종류의 옷이 당신에게 가장 잘 맞는지를 알아야 한다. 둘째, 옷을 선택할 때 의미(생각)를 부여해야 한다. 왜냐하면 당신이 입는 것은 종종 다른 사람들이 당신을 어떻게 보는가와 당신이 자신에 대해서 어떻게 느끼고 있는지에 영향을 주기 때문이다. 셋째, 현재 패션의 유행이 무엇인지 알고 당신의 옷장에서 무엇을 그대로 두고 무엇을 갱신할 것인지를 정하라.

3 당신의 옷을 갱신할 때라는 것을 어떻게 알 수 있는가? 옷장에 구매한지 10년 이나 그 이상 된 옷이 있는지 점검하라. 그것들이 당신이 아주 좋아하는 것이 아니라면 지금이 옷장을 정리할 때다. 그리고 나서 당신이 좋아하는 스타일에 대해 자세히 생각해 보라. 이것이 당신의 개인 이미지를 향상시키는 시작이다. 다음으로 당신이 어떤 유형의 옷을 입기가 편한지, 어떤 종류의 옷이 당신을 멋있게 보이게 하는지 생각해 보라. 마지막으로 유행이 지난 옷이나 당신의 생활방식에 더 이상 맞지 않는 옷을 버리라.

4 색상도 생각해 봐야 하는 것이다. 왜냐하면 그것은 당신의 이미지에 큰 부분을 차지하기 때문이다. 당신에게 어떤 색이 어울리는지 찾고 그 색상들 중심으로 옷장을 구성해보라. 이것은 당신이 선택한 옷을 섞어서 (색과 스타일을) 맞추는데 도움을 줄 것이다. 그 후에 서로 잘 맞는 옷들을 찾기 위해 옷을 새로운 조합으로 시도해 보라. 또한 반드시 무엇이 필요한지를 알아본 후에 그것을 사러 쇼핑을 가라. 당신의 체형과 사이즈에 맞춰서 옷을 사는 것을 기억하라. 예를 들면 스타일을 선택할 때 넓고 뚱뚱하게 보이게 하는 가로줄은 피하고 그 대신, 키가 더 크고 더 날씬하게 보이는 세로줄 무늬를 고려하라.

5 마지막으로 당신이 일을 하고 있으면 (직장상황에)알맞게 입을 필요가 있다. 검은 색은 사무직 근무자들에게 기본이다. 대안으로는 회색, 감청색 또는 다른 어두운 색상들이 좋다. 당신이 무엇을 입든 간에 그것은 당신에 관한 것을 말해주고 있고 다른 사람이 당신에 대해 보기를 원하는 이미지를 말하고 있음을 잊지 말라. 당신이 입고 있는 것은 당신에 관한 작은 부분을 다른 사람에게 알리는 기회이다. 그래서 일반적 규칙처럼 '(깊은)인상을 주기 위해서 (옷을)입어라'.

Translation

Lesson 4 AN AMERICAN WHO WAS MORE KOREAN THAN KOREANS

1 충청남도 태안에 위치한 천리포 수목원은 세계에서 가장 아름다운 정원들 중 하나로 알려져 있다. 수목원은 다양한 종류의 희귀하고 이국적인 나무와 꽃 들로 가득 차 있다. 놀랍게도 한국에서 이토록 귀중한 자연 환경은 한국에서 57년 동안 거주한 미국인에 의해 조성되었다.

2 칼 밀러는 미국 펜실베니아에서 1921년에 태어났다. 그는 1945년에 미국 해군의 일원으로 한국에 왔다. 오래지 않아 그는 한국의 경치를 사랑하게 되었다. 1952년에 밀러는 해군에서 제대하고 한국은행에 취직했다. 그는 매주 등산을 했다. 어느 날 그는 스님들로부터 우연히 한국의 식물에 대해 알게 되었다. 그 후는 그는 한국의 꽃과 나무를 기르는 데 관심을 갖게 되었다.

3 1962년에 밀러는 천리포를 처음 방문한 후 정원을 지을 땅을 샀다. 그 후 30년간 그는 자신의 모든 시간과 돈을 들여 정원을 가꾸었다. 산과 들을 헤매며 야생초와 야생화를 채집하였다. 또한 외국으로부터 새로운 종의 씨앗을 들여오기도 했다. 정원은 점점 더 커졌고, 마침내 1972년에 밀러는 천리포 수목원을 설립하였다.

4 오래지 않아 천리포 수목원은 전세계적으로 유명해졌다. 마침내 2000년에는 아시아에서 최초로 "세계에서 아름다운 수목원" 상을 수상하였다. 사람들은 수목원을 몹시 방문하고 싶어했지만, 밀러는 수목원을 대중에게 개방하지 않았다. 수목원의 자연 환경을 보존하고 싶었기 때문이었다.

5 여러모로 밀러는 한국인들 보다 더 한국적이었다. 그는 종종 "내가 한국을 사랑하는 것은 아마도 내가 전생에 한국인이었기 때문일 거라 생각한다." 말했다고 전해진다. 그는 한옥집에 살며 한복을 즐겨 입고 김치를 즐겨 먹었다. 1979년에 그는 결국 한국으로 귀화하여 민병갈이라는 한국이름도 갖게 되었다. 그는 2002년 81세의 나이에 암으로 사망했다.

6 현재 천리포 수목원은 대중에게 개방되어 있다. 그 곳에는 7000여종의 토종과 외래종 식물들이 자라고 있다. 매년 수천 명의 사람들이 방문해 민병갈이 평생을 헌신해서 이룬 수목원의 자연적 아름다움을 즐긴다.

Lesson 5 A CHEROKEE WOMAN WHO MADE A DIFFERENCE

1 2010년 4월6일 윌마 맨킬러라는 64세의 체로키 여성이 암으로 사망하였다. 이 소식을 듣고 많은 미국인들은 깊은 슬픔에 빠졌다. 심지어 오바마 대통령 조차 그녀의 죽음에 대해 애도를 표했다. 무엇이 이토록 많은 사람들이 이 여성의 죽음을 슬퍼하게 만들었는가?

2 윌마 맨킬러는 1945년 오클라호마의 작은 마을인 타레콰에서 출생했다. 그녀의 이름 맨킬러는 그녀의 고조 할아버지에서 이어 받은 것으로 체로키 마을을 수호하는 전사라는 뜻이다. 그녀의 집안은 가난해서 전기도 수도도 없이 살아야만 했다. 하지만 윌마는 행복했다. 그녀는 책읽기를 좋아하고 다른 체로키 아이들과 노는 것을 즐겼다.

3 그녀가 12살이 되었을 때 상황은 갑자기 달라졌다. 미국정부가 실행한 아메리컨 인디언들을 도시로 이주시키는 정책 때문에 가족이 샌프란시스코로 이사를 가게 된 것이었다. 그녀는 그곳에서 중학교에 들어 갔는데 학교생활은 행복하지 않았다. 대부분이 백인인 그녀의 반 친구들은 그녀의 이름과 그녀가 인디언이라는 사실을 조롱했기 때문이었다.

4 학교에서의 이런 경험은 윌마가 체로키 인디언들의 권리를 위한 운동에 참여하는 데 중요한 역할을 했다. 1969년 아메리컨 인디언에 대한 부당한 대우에 대해 항의하기 위해 일단의 인디언 학생들이 샌프란시스코 근처에 있는 알카트라즈라는 섬을 점거하는 사태가 벌어졌다. 윌마는 이 소식을 듣고 이 점거 농성에 참여했다. 이 일을 겪은 후 윌마는 체로키 인디언의 복지를 개선하는 데 헌신하기로 결심하고 1977년 오클라호마로 돌아왔다.

5 오클라호마에서 윌마는 체로키 인디언들의 생활환경을 개선시키기 위해 열심히 일했다. 그 결과 새로운 수도시설들이 만들어지고 낡은 주택들은 재건축되었다. 곧 그녀의 성공담은 미국 전역에 알려지고 윌마는 유명인사가 되었다.

6 이러한 성공에도 불구하고 윌마는 많은 어려움을 겪어야만 했다. 1979년에는 자동차 사고를 당하게 심하게 다쳤다. 또한 암에 걸려 투병하기도 했다. 하지만. 윌마는 이 모든 시련을 극복하고 1985년 체로키인디언 대추장직에 출마하였다. 하지만, 많은 체로키 사람들은 단지 그녀가 여자라는 이유로 그녀가 추장이 되는 것을 원하지 않았다. 어떤 사람들은 그녀를 죽이겠다고 협박하기도 했다. 이러한 어려움에도 불구하고 윌마는 마침내 체로키 역사상 최초의 여성 추장이 되었다.

7 윌마가 대추장이 된 후 체로키는 엄청난 발전을 이루었다. 인구가 증가하고, 더 많은 사람들이 직장을 얻게 되었고, 새로운 의료 진료소와 아동들을 위한 프로그램들이 만들어졌다. 윌마는 체로키 언어와 전통을 보존하기 위해서도 열심히 일했다. 이제 그녀는 아메리칸 인디언의 삶을 변화시킨 위대한 지도자도 기억되고 있다.

Translation

Lesson 6 VOICES OF HYCU STUDENTS

나의 삶은 끔직히 바쁘다. 35살의 엄마이고, 아내이며, 전임 영어강사이며 한양사이버대학교의 학생이다. 사람들은 나를 수퍼맘이라고 부르는데 이젠 나도 정말 그렇다고 생각하기 시작했다. 나는 직장에서 7시에 퇴근하여 집에 오면 집안일을 한다. 그리고 나서 노트북을 켜고, 나의 딸아이, 예린이를 무릎에 앉히고 공부를 한다. 거의 대부분 자정이 넘어서까지 깨어있다. 내 남편은 왜 내가 공부에 그렇게 몰두하는지 궁금해하는데 나는 나름의 이유가 있다. 대학원에 진학하고 싶다는 것, 쉽지는 않겠지만 나의 결심은 확고하다. 내 딸이 나에게 빵을 가져다 주며 말한다. "엄마, 이거 먹고 공부 열심히 해요!", 내 딸의 격려는 항상 나를 전진하게 하는 큰 힘이 된다.

내 주위사람들은 내가 성공했다고들 한다. 제조회사의 사장이니 아마도 맞는 말일지도 모르겠다. 지난 30년간, 나는 내 꿈을 아주 많이 이루었다. 나의 가장 큰 성취 중 하나는 나의 51살에 영어공부를 하기 위해 한양사이버대학교에 입학한 것이다. 한양사이버대학교에서 학생들만이 할 수 있는 경험들을 다양하게 즐길 기회가 있었다. 나는 학교 과외활동에 참여하였고, 많은 어린 친구들을 사귀게 되었고, 영어말하기대회에서 일등을 하기도 하고, 물론 공부도 매우 열심히 하였다. 결국, 나는 학사 학위를 3년 반 만에 취득할 수 있었고, 심리학 전공으로 대학원에 진학하였다. 지금은, 만만치 않은 대학원과정 수업을 듣느라 매우 바쁘다. 그러는 동안, 나는 박사과정을 위한 공부를 계속하기 위한 새로운 계획을 세웠다. 누가 알겠나, 미래 한양사이버대학교의 교수가 될 지!

내 삶은 언제나 도전으로 가득하다. 한양사이버대학교에 입학하기 전, 나는 오프라인 대학교에서 2학년을 마치고 대한민국공군에 입대해 항공관제사로 일하였다. 나의 임무는 파일럿들의 안전을 위해 항공 교통 상황을 영어로 안내하는 것이었다. 어느 날, 사이버대에서는 공군에서 일을 하면서 학사 학위를 받을 수 있다는 것을 알게 되었다. 오랜 고민 끝에, 다니던 대학을 자퇴하고 한양사이버대학교에 편입하기로 결심하였다. 그것은 매우 잘한 결정이었다. 한양사이버대학교에서 배운 모든 것은 나의 영어 실력을 향상시키는데 도움이 되었고, 더 나아가게 고취시켜 주었다. 몇 달 뒤에는 어학연수를 위해 미국에 갈 것이다. 그 후에 나는 국제 공항에서 일하는 내 자신을 상상해본다.

사람들은 자주 왜 내 나이에 영어를 공부하는지 물어본다. 10년 동안 피아노 강사를 하다 50살이 되어 무엇인가 새로운 것을 시작한다는 것은 쉬운 결정은 아니었다. 하지만 나는 늘 영어로 소설을 쓰고 싶었고 한양사이버대학교야말로 내가 영어실력을 키울 수 있는 이상적인 곳이라고 생각했다. 나는 배운 단어를 기억하는 것이 특히 어려워 늘 사전에서 단어를 찾는다. 그건 시간이 오래 걸리고 때론 고통스럽기까지 하다. 하지만 나는 영어를 공부하는 매 순간을 즐긴다. 왜냐하면 내 영어실력이 나아지는 것이 보이기 때문이다. 한양사이버대학교에서 내 꿈을 향해 공부하는 것은 나에게 젊음과 활력소가 된다.

Lesson 9 LANGUAGE LEARNING FACTORS

1 "새들은 왜 계속해서 노래를 부르나요?" 이것은 "세상의 끝" 이라는 제목의 오래된 미국 팝송 가사의 일부분이다. 비록 사랑에 관한 내용이지만 이 노래는 흥미로운 질문을 던진다: 애초에, 새들은 왜, 어떤 방법으로 노래를 부르는가? 전문가들에 의하면, 일부 새들은 그들이 새끼일 때 어른 새들로부터 노래 부르는 법을 배운다고 한다. 따라서 만약 새들이 (이 시기에) 노래를 배울 수 있는 기회를 놓친다면, 그들은 나중에 노래를 배우려고 해도 상당한 어려움이 있을 것이라고 한다. 사람들은 이러한 시기를 "결정적 시기" 라고 부른다. 더 중요한 점은, 일부 언어 전문가들에 따르면, 이 결정적 시기가 인간에게도 적용될 수 있다고 주장한다는 점이다. 언어를 습득하는데 필요한 다른 가능한 요인들과 더불어 말이다.

2 인간에게도 결정적 시기가 존재할 수 있다는 것을 보여주는 전형적인 예가 "지니" 라는 이름의 한 소녀에게서 발견된다. 그녀는 1970년 캘리포니아에서 13살의 나이로 발견되었으나 "그만해" 와 같은 짧은 구들을 제외하고는 말할 수가 없었다. 지니는 발견되기 전, 어둡고 문이 잠긴 방에서 혼자 살았었다. 거의 어느 누구도 – 심지어는 지니의 부모님조차도 – 지니와 자주 만나거나 대화를 나누지 않았다. 그 결과, (발견 된 후) 언어 전문가들이 지니에게 영어를 가르쳐 주려고 노력을 하였지만 지니는 단지 100개 정도의 단어들만 배울 수 있었고 그 이상의 진전은 없었다.

3 지니의 경우는 모국어 습득에 관한 것인데, 외국어 습득은 어떻게 이루어지는 것인가? 성공적인 외국어 습득이 이루어지기 위해서는 우리들도 어릴 때부터 영어를 배우기 시작해야 될까? 일반적으로 언어 전문가들은 외국어를 습득하기 위해서는 나이가 어리면 어릴수록 더 좋다고 믿는 편이다. 더 구체적으로, 모국어에 근접하는 유창성을 기르기 위해서는 사춘기가 시작되기 전에 외국어를 배워야 한다고 말한다.

4 그러나 연구결과들에 따르면 외국어를 습득하는데 있어서 다른 요인들도 또한 중요하다고 한다. 바로 배우고자 하는 동기와 시간투자가 그 예들이다. 즉, 어떤 사람이 영어를 배우고자 하는 동기가 높고 시간도 충분히 투자를 한다면 그 사람의 영어실력은 향상될 수 있다. 물론 나이가 어린 학습자일수록 더 유창하게, 더 좋은 발음으로 해당 언어를 구사할 수 있겠지만 나이가 든 학습자라도 (동기부여가 되어 있고 충분한 시간투자를 한다면) 큰 어려움 없이 언어를 배울 수 있고 의사소통이 가능할 수 있다.

5 사실은 (유창하고 좋은 발음의 영어보다는) 성공적으로 의사소통 할 수 있는 능력이 더 중요하다. 일부 새들과 사람들에게 결정적 시기가 적용될 수도 있겠지만 여전히 희망은 있다. 만약 우리가 최선의 노력을 계속 한다면 우리는 더 훌륭한 영어를 구사할 수 있고 성공적인 의사소통도 가능할 것이다. 그러니 포기하지 마라. (결정적 시기 또는 외국어를 배우기 시작한 나이 외에도) 본인의 하고자 하는 동기와 시간투자도 중요하다는 것을 잊어서는 안 된다.

Translation

Lesson 10 BODY LANGUAGE DIFFERS ACROSS CULTURES

1 "의사소통" 에 대해 이야기할 때, 가장 먼저 생각나는 것은 아마도 한 사람이 말을 하는 것이고, 다른 사람이 듣는 것일 것이다. 즉, 말하는 것은 의사소통을 하는 데 있어서 가장 중요한 방법인 것처럼 생각된다. 하지만 전문가들에 의하면 우리 대화의 절반 이상이 사실은 몸짓 언어를 통해 전달된다고 한다. 전문가들은 주장하기를, 이 조용한 언어는 말로 의사소통을 하는 것만큼 중요하며, 그 이유는 몸짓 언어는 그것 나름대로의 의미들을 가지고 있고, 이러한 의미들은 문화들마다 또한 다를 수 있기 때문이다.

2 손을 이용한 동작들이 그 전형적인 예이다. 한국에서는 누군가에게 "여기로 오세요" 라는 신호를 줄 때, 손바닥을 아래를 보도록 향하게 한 뒤 손가락을 앞뒤로 움직인다. 하지만 미국식의 "여기로 오세요"를 뜻하는 방식은 한국식과는 정반대이다. 손바닥을 위로 향하게 하고 손가락을 동시에 앞뒤로 움직이는데, 이 동작은 아이들이나 동물들에게 사용될 수 있다. 비슷하게 한국에서도 이 손동작이 사용되지만 애완동물을 부를 때만 사용한다. 따라서 만약 (한국에서) 사람들에게 이 손동작을 사용한다면 그것은 굉장히 무례하게 받아들여 질 수 있다.

3 (몸짓 언어의) 또 다른 예는 특정 머리 동작이다. 한국을 포함한 대부분의 나라에서 사람들은 머리를 위 아래로 끄덕이면서 "예" 를 표현한다. "아니오" 를 표현하기 위해서는 머리를 좌우로 흔든다. 그러나 세계의 일부 지역에서는 이러한 동작들을 반대로 사용한다. 그리스, 유고슬라비아, 불가리아, 그리고 터키의 일부 지역에서는 머리를 좌우로 흔들면서 "예" 를 표현하고 위 아래로 끄덕이면서 "아니오" 를 나타낸다. 따라서 만약 당신이 이러한 지역들 중 한 곳으로 여행하게 된다면 이런 다른 점을 기억해 두는 것이 좋다.

4 몸짓 언어는 항상 손과 머리처럼 몸의 부분에 관한 것만은 아니다. 개인 공간 또한 (문화에 따라서는) 다른 의미를 나타낼 수 있는 몸짓 언어에 속한다. 예를 들어, 미국에서 사람들은 서로에게 너무 가까이 서 있지 않는다. 서로가 편안하게 느끼는 공간(comfort zone)을 침범하지 않기 위한 이유이다. 하지만 만약 당신이 스페인에 가게 된다면, 스페인들에게는 이런 개인 공간이라는 개념이 없다는 것을 발견하게 될 것이다. (따라서) 스페인에서는 다음의 재미있는 장면을 볼 수 있다. 미국인과 스페인 사람이 대화를 나눌 때, 미국인이 좀 더 편안함을 느끼기 위해서 스페인 사람에게서 뒤로 물러서게 되면, 그 스페인 사람은 거리를 (다시) 좁히기 위해서 사실 앞으로 더 다가가는 장면을 말이다!

5 요약하면, 몸짓 언어는 단어들처럼 그것만의 의미들을 가지고 있다. 그 의미들은 또한 문화마다 다르다. 따라서 당신이 만약 외국으로 여행을 갈 예정이라면, 그 나라의 몸짓 언어를 확실히 배워두는 것이 좋다. 방문국의 몸짓 언어에 대한 지식은 당신의 여행을 즐겁게 만들거나 불만족스러운 경험으로 만들 수 있다. 가끔은 "행동이(몸짓언어가) 말보다 더 중요하다" 라는 말을 기억해라.

1 "화성에서 온 남자, 금성에서 온 여자" 는 1992년에 출판된 존 그레이 저서의 책이다. 자신의 책에서 존은 남자와 여자는 다른 사고방식을 가지고 있기 때문에 대화방식 또한 다르다고 설명한다. 이러한 차이점들은 너무 커서 이 두 집단은 마치 두 개의 다른 행성에서 온 것처럼 묘사된다! 많은 연구자들은 이러한 성으로 인한 차이점들이 어떤 식으로 북미 문화권의 영어사용에 반영되어 있는지 연구해 왔다.

2 미국 대학 교수인 데보라 태넌의 설명에 따르면, 어릴 때부터 남자 아이들과 여자 아이들은 다른 방식으로 행동하고 대화한다고 한다. 예를 들어, 남자 아이들이 놀이를 할 때, 그들은 서로 경쟁을 하면서 그들 집단에서 우두머리가 되려고 노력한다. 반대로 여자 아이들이 놀이를 할 때는, 협동적인 환경을 만듦으로써 서로간의 친목을 형성하려고 노력한다. 이런 행동은 아이들의 언어 사용에도 나타난다. (즉,) 남자 아이들은 명령문과 같은 형태의 권위적인 언어를 자주 사용하는 편이고, 여자 아이들은, 예를 들자면, "~하자" 로 끝나는 좀 더 협동적인 언어를 사용한다고 한다.

3 이러한 성에 따른 차이점은 성인들의 대화에서도 나타난다. 태넌이 발견하기를, 남자들이 여자들로부터 불평을 들을 때, 남자들은 해결방법을 제시해 주려고 한다. 그러나 여자들이 본인들의 문제들에 대해 이야기를 할 때는, 상대방이 그저 들어 주고 감정을 공유해 주기를 바랄 뿐이다. 이렇게 함으로써 여자들은 상대방과 좀 더 친밀해짐을 느끼는 것이다. (성으로 인한 언어사용의 차이점의) 다른 예는 여성이 남자에게 차를 멈추고 커피 한잔 하고 싶은지 물을 때, 마시고 싶지 않은 남자의 경우, 바로 "난 괜찮아" 라고 대답할 것이다. 그럼 여자의 입장에서는 자신의 의견이 무시되었다는 생각이 들면서 기분이 언짢아 질 수가 있다. 그럼 남자는 그가 무엇을 잘못한 건지 이해할 수 없게 되고 (역시) 답답해 할 것이다.

4 성과 언어라는 주제에 관해, 연구자들은 성 편견으로 인한 단어들이 영어에 존재함을 또한 알아냈다. 물론 이러한 단어들을 중립화 시키기 위한 노력들이 있어 왔지만 말이다. 예를 들어, 과거에 대명사 "he"는 남자 또는 여자를 지칭하기 위해 사용되었다. (하지만) 오늘날에는 "he or she" 또는 "people"이 더 자주 사용된다. 비슷한 예로, "man" 이란 단어는 과거에 "people" 을 의미할 수 있었지만 현재는 "people" 또는 "human beings" 란 단어들이 선호된다. 이 외에도 혼인여부를 나타내는 것에 있어서 "Mr." 는 기혼남 또는 미혼남을 의미할 수 있다. 하지만 여자들의 경우에는 결혼여부를 좀 더 구체적으로 나타내기 위해 "Miss" 또는 "Mrs." 중 하나를 사용해야 했다. (하지만) 오늘날에는 "Mr." 처럼 "Ms." 가 사용되어 기혼녀 또는 미혼녀를 의미한다. 다른 성 편견으로 인한 단어들의 예에는 "chairman" 과 "businessman" 이 있다.

5 요약하면, 성과 언어라는 주제는 매우 흥미로운 내용으로 많은 것을 알고 싶게 만드는 주제 같다. 만약 우리들이 남자와 여자의 서로 다른 사고방식과 대화방식을 이해하고 그 이유 또한 이해한다면, 반대 성의 사람들과의 소통은 더 쉬워질 것이고 훨씬 더 부드러운 관계를 유지할 수 있을 것이다.

Lesson 12 A FOREIGNER'S EXPERIENCES IN KOREA

1 매년 점점 더 많은 외국인들이 방문하기 위해, 일하기 위해, 또는 거주하기 위해 한국을 여행한다. 그들의 다수는 블로그를 이용하여 한국에 대한 경험을 공유하고 있다. 제니퍼도 그런 사람들 중 하나다.

한옥에서 지내기

2 지난 주말, 나는 전주에 여행가서 한옥에 머물렀다. 처음에는 딱딱한 바닥에서 자는 것에 대해 조금 걱정하였으나, 나는 정말로 잘 잤고 아침에 내 허리는 멀쩡했다. 나는 한옥에 대해서 몇 가지 장점을 발견하였다. 우선 바닥은 온돌을 통해 아주 잘 데워지는데, 온돌이란 불에 의해 가열되고 나무 판으로 덮어진 전통적인 돌 바닥이다. 창은 공기의 흐름을 더 좋게 하는 한국 전통 종이로 만들어져서, 방안의 공기는 상쾌하다. 벽은 진흙으로 만들어졌는데 상당히 두툼하여, 내 방이 길에 면한 1층이었는데도 아무 소리도 들리지 않았다. 아침엔, 집주인 아줌마가 된장찌개-뜨겁게 끓인 콩소스 스튜, 구운 고등어와 다른 많은 밑반찬으로 된 전주의 전형적인 아침 식사를 차려 주었다. 미국에서는 아침에 커피한 잔 정도 마시던 나에겐 확실히 특별한 경험이었다. 하지만, 이틀 묵은 경험이 매우 좋았다는 것을 인정하지만, 집에 돌아가 내 침대로 돌아가게 되어 행복하다.

광장시장

3 오늘, 나는 광장시장을 방문했다. 나에게 진짜 한국의 길거리 시장에 가는 것은 처음이다. 내 모국에서 길거리 시장에 가는 것이 익숙하기 때문에, 한국에서도 비슷할 것이라고 생각했다. 그러나 한국의 길거리 시장은 내가 예상한 것과 상당히 다르다는 것을 알게 되었다.

4 시장에 들어서자마자, 한복 섹션, 농산물 지역과 수산물 지역 그리고 섬유 섹션과 같은 많은 종류의 다른 섹션을 보게 되어 매우 놀랐다. 내가 가장 좋았던 것은 신선한 생선과, 야채, 떡, 김밥 등을 팔고 있는 가판이었다. 그것이 너무 맛있게 보이고 맛있는 냄새가 나서 다른 종류의 음식들을 먹지 않을 수가 없었다. 정말 맛있었고 더군다나 믿을 수 없이 저렴했다. 팥죽 한 접시가 단돈 4000원인데, 보통 식당의 절반 가격이었다. 그리고 상인은 돈도 받지 않고 덤을 주었다. 내가 다 먹었을 무렵에는 너무 배가 불러 숨을 쉬기 어려울 정도였다!

5 그 후에는 한복 가게들을 둘러보았고, 그곳 사람들은 내가 아름다운 한복을 입어보도록 허락해주었다. 거울을 봤을 때, 의상이 나를 천사처럼 보이도록 만들었다고 생각했다. 나는 너무 흥분해서 바닥에 전통인사를 하려고 하다가 넘어졌고, 내 주변 사람들은 모두 웃음을 터뜨렸다. 나는 조금 창피했지만 괜찮았다. 한국의 문화의 독특한 면을 경험할 수 있는 지역을 즐겁고 재미있게 거닌 것이다.

Lesson 13 HOLIDAYS AROUND THE WORLD

1 모든 문화는 특별한 날을 축하하는 그들 각각의 독특한 방법이 있다. 여기에서 전세계의 다른 축하에 대해서 설명하겠다.

멕시코의 죽은자의 날

2 언뜻 보면, 죽은 자의 날 슬픈 행사처럼 들릴지도 모르지만 실제로는 멕시코의 축제이다. 이 행복한 가족 이벤트는 10월 31일과 11 월 2 일 사이에 사흘 동안 지속된다. 이 기간 동안 멕시코는 그들의 조상을 기억하고 존중하는 시간이 갖는다. 첫째 날은, 가족들은 죽은 친척의 무덤을 방문한다. 그들은 꽃과 흙, 촛불로 무덤가를 장식한다. 둘째 날에는 가족들은 함께 모여 조상들이 좋아했던 음식을 준비한다. 곳에 따라서는 무덤에서 밤을 보내기도 한다. 밤새, 파티를 열고, 음식을 나누어먹고, 음악을 연주하고 이야기 하고 마신다. 마지막 날, 마을 사람들 전부가 마스크와 의상을 입고 퍼레이드에 참석하는 축제에 동참한다. 심지어 의상 콘테스트가 있기도 하다. 이 축제는 한 해의 수확에 대한 감사하는 의미로 시작되었으나, 이제는 추모와 기념의 날이다.

스페인의 새해

3 스페인 사람들은 설날의 자정에 포도 12알을 먹는 풍습이 있는데, 시계종 하나에 한 개씩을 먹는다. 그들은 각 포도알이 그 해의 달을 상징한다고 믿었다. 그들이 먹는 각각의 달콤한 포도알은 좋은 달이 될 것이며, 각 신 포도알은 나쁜 달이 될 것이다. 예를 들어, 두 번째 포도알이 시다면, 두 번째 달, 2월이 불운한 한 달이 될 것이다. 그렇기 때문에 그들은 모든 포도알이 달기를 바란다. 그리고 그들은 12번의 시계종이 치기 전에 모든 포도알을 먹으려고 하는데 새해에 행운이 있을 것이라고 믿기 때문이다. 이 풍습은 1909년에 스페인에서 포도 풍년을 축하하기 위해 시작되었다. 스페인의 왕은 새해 전날에 자신의 모든 국민들에게 포도를 주었다.

인도의 빛의 축제

4 DIWALI 또는 빛의 축제는 힌두교의 가장 중요한 휴일 중 하나입니다. 그것은 힌두교의 음력달의 마지막 이틀과 첫 이틀 사이에 (9월에서 10월까지) 축하행사이다. 힌두교 부의 여신인, 락쉬미를 받을 램프나 촛불로 집을 밝힌다. 그들은 이 기간 동안 이 여신이 그녀의 시골집에서 돌아와 그 램프로 그녀의 길을 찾는데 도움을 받을 것이라고 믿는다. 사람들은 락쉬미를 위해 기도 하면 행운을 가져다 주고, 불을 밝히지 않은 집은 축복하지 않을 것이라고 믿는다. DIWALI도 또한 힌두교의 새해의 시작이다. 새해의 시작을 환영하기 위해, 사람들은 집을 청소하고, 그들 친구와 친척 들을 초대하여, 그들의 삶에서 분노, 증오, 그리고 질투를 없애기 위해 서로를 격려한다.

Translation

Lesson 14 THE KOREAN WAVE: PAST, PRESENT AND FUTURE

1 "한류"또는 KOREAN WAVE는 1990년대 중반 중국 기자들이 최초 만들어 낸 문구이다. 그 이후로 한국 엔터테인먼트는 세계적인 돌풍이 되었다. 한류는 처음에 일본, 중국, 태국 등 여러 아시아 국가에서 몇몇 한국 TV 프로와 영화가 방영되면서 시작되었다. 가장 최근 한류의 인기는 K-팝 음악과 온라인 게임을 포함하여 성장하였는데, 유럽과 미국으로 확산되었다. 이젠 그들이 좋아하는 한국 스타를 보기 위해 국제 공항에 나타나 열렬히 기다리는 거대 팬 그룹을 보는 것은 놀랄 일이 아니다.

2 여러 가지 면에서, 한류는 한국에 경제적 또는 문화적으로 크게 득이 되고 있다. 예를 들어, 전세계에서 오는 수백만의 관광객들이 한국을 방문하여, 그들이 좋아하는 쇼 또는 영화들의 촬영 장소를 방문한다. 2011년을 예를 들면, 40만 관광객이 남이섬을 방문하였는데, 그곳은 "겨울 연가"를 촬영했던 곳이다. 또한, K-팝 음악 그룹과 가수는 그들의 팬에게 큰 영향을 미치는데, 특히 음식, 패션, 메이크업 트렌드, 심지어 성형 수술 등이다. 결과적으로, 한국 제품은 전세계의 많은 사람들에게 "MUST-HAVE(꼭가져야하는)" 아이템이 되었다. 더군다나 많은 외국인들이 한국 문화를 알고 싶어하고 있다. 사실, 많은 사람들이 외국어로서의 한국어 학습에 관심을 보이고 있다. 한국어를 배우러 한국에 오는 학생들도 점점 늘고 있다.

3 이런 세계적인 인기에도 불구하고, 한국은 장차 한류의 성공을 지속할 수 없을 것이라고 경고하는 사람들이 있다. 최근 조사에 따르면, 많은 사람들이 최근 한국 문화에 대한 높은 관심이 지속되지 않을 것이라고 생각한다. 사실, 어떤 외국인들은 같은 것을 보고 또 보는 것에 지겨워지고 있다. 예를 들면, 어떤 이들은 다양한 K-POP 가수가 비슷한 타입의 옷을 입고, 비슷한 춤동작을 하고, 비슷한 노래 가사를 사용하는 것을 지적한다. 한국 드라마 또한 주제가 삼각관계와 복수를 반복하는 것에 초점이 맞춰져 있다고 비판 받는다. 일본과 같은 일부 국가에서는, 한류에 대한 적대감도 생기고 있다. 일부 일본인들은 한국 프로를 방송하는 방송국에 항의를 하고 있다. 전문가들은 지금은 변화할 때라고 지적한다.

4 다행히 한국은 이러한 도전에 대응하고 있다. 일부 한국 연예 산업은 인터넷 기술과 소셜 미디어, 이를테면 유투브와 SMS 사이트들을 한류를 위한 새로운 원동력으로 사용하기 시작했다. 또한 한국 정부는 다양한 문화적 행사와 다른 나라들과의 국제적인 협력을 추진하며 한류를 부양하기 위해 손쓰기 시작했다. 한류를 확장하고 유지하는 것은 쉬운 일은 아니지만, 한국은 모든 방면의 이미지를 개선하기 위해 홍보하는 노력을 계속해야 한다.

Vocabulary List

1차시

such as	..와 같은
consider	고려하다
carbohydrate	탄수화물
chew	씹다
consume	먹다, 마시다
contain	포함하다
cut down on	줄이다
disease	질병
essential	필수적인
grocery	식료품
illness	질병
improve	향상시키다
include	포함하다
increase	증가하다
intake	섭취, 섭취량
maintain	유지하다
meal	끼니
meat	고기
nutrients	영양소
plate	접시
portion	(음식의)1인분
poultry	가금류
prevent	예방하다
protein	단백질
recipe	조리법
risk	위험
salmon	연어
smart	똑똑한
start off	시작하다
take time	시간을두고 천천히하다
tip	조언
when it comes to	..에관해서는
whole grain	통곡물
reduce	줄이다
grain	곡물

2차시

abdominal	복부의
aerobic	유산소의
allow	허락하다
amount	양, 액수
based on	..에 근거하여
benefit	이득
breathing	숨쉬기
burn	태우다
chest	흉부
chore	잡일
crunch	윗몸굽히기
deliver	전하다
effectiveness	유효성
flexibility	유연성
gymnastics	체조
household	집안의
in addition to	..에 더하여
in general	일반적으로
injury	부상
instead of	.. 대신에
involve	포함하다
joint	관절
leg raise	다리들어 올리기
mass	질량
muscle	근육
overweight	과체중
oxygen	산소
physical	신체의
plenty of	많은
prefer	좋아하다
pull-up	턱걸이
push-up	팔굽혀 펴기
reduce	줄이다
sit-up	윗몸일으키기
squat	(다리를)웅크리기
stairs	계단
strengthen	강화하다
workout	신체활동/운동

3차시

according to	..에 의하면
appear	..처럼보이다
appropriately	상황에 어울리게
avoid	피하다
closet	벽장
clothes	옷
clothing	의류
combination	조합
comfort	편안, 안락
comfortable	편안한
current	현재의
favorite	특히 좋아하는것
find out	알아보다
fit	(치수가)꼭 맞는
get rid of	제거하다
horizontal	가로의
identity	정체성
item	품목
look good on	어울리는
match	어울리다
offer	제공하다
opportunity	기회
organize	정리하다
out of date	구식의
outfit	복장, 도구의 한 벌
personal	개인적인
prepare	분비하다
protection	보호
stripes	줄무늬
stylish	멋진, 유행을따르는
trend	유행
update	새롭게하다
vertical	세로의
wardrobe	옷장

4차시

afterward	나중에
anxious	갈망하는
Arboretum	수목원
award	상을 수여하다
become interested in	에 관심을 갖게 되다
build	건설하다
collect	수집하다
currently	현재
devotion	헌신
die of	로 사망하다
entire	전체의
environment	환경
establish	설립하다
eventually	궁극적으로
fall in love with	와 사랑에 빠지다
famous	유명한
finally	마침내
happen to	우연히 ..하다
herb	풀
is known as	로 알려져 있다
monk	수도사
natural	자연의
navy	해군
past	과거
plant	식물
preserve	보존하다
previous	과거
public	공공의
quote	인용하다
raise	기르다
rare	드문
seed	씨앗
species	(식물이나 동물의)종
valuable	가치있는
various	다양한
wander	방황하다
worldwide	전세계적으로

5차시

against	에 반대하여
challenge	도전
deep	깊은
despite	에도 불구하고

Vocabulary List

electricity	전기
experience	경험
female	여성
go through	겪다
government	정부
hardship	어려움
health center	보건소
injure	상처를 입히다
island	섬
make fun of	놀리다
mourn	애도하다
move	이사가다
occupy	점령하다
overcome	극복하다
participate in	에 참여하다
population	인구
Pricipal chief	대추장
progress	발전
protest	항의하다
relocate	재배치 시키다
remember	기억하다
run for	에 출마하다
sadness	슬픔
seriously	심각하게
success	성공
suffer from	로 고통을 겪다
threaten	위협하다
tradition	전통
treatment	대우
unfair	부당한
warrior	전사
welfare	복지

6차시

After long thought	오랜 생각 끝에
air traffic controller	관제사
branch	지사
bread	빵
communicate	의사소통하다
competition	경쟁
decision	결정
dictionary	사전
disappointing	실망스러운
do one's best	최선을 다하다
encouragement	격려
energetic	활기 찬
energize	힘이나게하다
explain	설명하다
extra-curricular	과외 활동
graduate school	대학원
housework	가사일
ideal	이상적인
lacking	부족한
laptop	노트북 컴퓨터
lecture	강의
look up	(사전등을) 찾아보다
manufacturing	제조업의
meanwhile	그동안
midnight	자정
novel	소설
painful	고통스러운
particularly	특히
prepare	준비하다
realize	깨닫다
reason	이유
strength	강점
succeed in	성공하다
take part in	에 참가하다
terribly	대단히
toward	을 향하여
translator	통역사
turn on	을 켜다

9차시

acquire	습득하다
age	나이
argue	주장하다
bird	새
by herself	혼자
commitment	투입
classic	고전적인
critical	매우 중요한
difficulty	문제/어려움
early	일찍
effort	노력
end up	결국 .. 하게 되다
existence	존재/실재
expert	전문가
factor	요인
fluent	유창한
go on	계속해서 .. 하다
human	인간/사람
in the first place	먼저/우선
lock	잠그다
lyrics	가사
make our best efforts	최선을 노력을 하다
miss	놓치다
motivation	자극/동기
parent	부모
period	시기/기간
possible	가능한
pronunciation	발음
puberty	사춘기

10차시

abroad	해외로
actually	사실은
American "come here" gesture	"여기 오세요" 신호
amusing	재미있는
back and forth	앞뒤로
backward	뒤로
call over	..을 부르다
convey	(생각, 감정등을) 전달하다
different	다른
downward	아래쪽을 향하여
face	..을 향하다
finger	손가락
forward	앞으로
go to	..로 가다
half	절반
in parts of	..의 일부 지역에서는
It seems that	..인 듯 생각되다
invade	침입하다
mind	머리
mistake	오해하다
more than	..이상의
nod	고개를 끄덕이다
notion	개념
opposite	정반대(의)
palm	손바닥
part	..의 일부, 부분
personal space	개인 공간
rude	무례한
space	공간
study	공부하다
typical	전형적인/대표적인
way	방법

11차시

adult	성인의
annoyed	짜증이 난, 약이 오른
are described as	..로 묘사되다
authoritative	권위적인
behave	행동하다
chairman	회의의 의장
childhood	어린 시절
command	명령어
compete	경쟁하다
compete with	..와 경쟁하다
complaint	불평
cooperative	협동하는
fascinating	대단히 흥미로운
for instance	예를 들어

frustrated 불만스러운
identify 알아보다/확인하다
ignore 무시하다
in contrast 반대로
indicate 나타내다/표현하다
instantly 즉시
intimate 매우 가까운
learn about ..에 대해 배우다
Mars 화성
married 결혼한
play 놀다/놀이를 하다
preference 선호
professor 교수
rapport 친밀감
researcher 연구자
solution 해결책
Venus 금성

12차시

a bit 약간
a coffee-for-breakfast type of person 커피를 아침 삼아 먹는 사람
additional 부가의
admit 인정한다
agricultural 농업의
allow 허용한다
amazing 놀라운
aspect 양상
assume ~라고 생각한다
back 등, 뒤에
bowl 그릇, 사발
breathe 숨쉬다
costume embarrassed 당황한
face -를 향한다
flow 흐름
ground floor 일층
hardly 거의- 않는
helping 한 사람 몫의 음식
incredibly 믿기 힘들게
laughter 웃음
looked in the mirror 거울을 들여다보다
marine products 해산물
merchant 상인
mud 진흙
noise 소음
on my return home 집으로 돌아와서
section 구획, 부분
similar 비슷한
sleep soundly 푹 자다
step into 로 걸어 들어가다

stroll 산책
stroll 산책
thick 두꺼운
worried 걱정이 된

13차시

ancestor 조상
anger 분노
attend 참여하다
bless 축복하다
celebration 축하생사
chime 종소리
custom 풍습
deceased 사망한
decorate 장식하다
fortune 행운
gather 모이다
goddess 여신
guide 안내하다
harvest 추수
hate 증오
honor 찬양하다
jealousy 질투
last 지속하다
lunar month 음력
occasion 행사
originally 원래
pray 기도하다
relative 친척
remembrance 추모
remove 제거하다
sour 맛이 신
stroke 시계 종이 치는 것
take time to ~ ~을 시간을 들여 하다
wealth 부

14차시

air 방송하다
appear 나타나다
benefit 득을 보다
broadcast 방영하다
coin 말을 만들다
cooperation 조
criticize 비판하다
drive engine 동력
expand 확대하다
expert 전문가
film 영화를 찍다
focus on -에 초점을 맞추다
hostility 적대감
Include 포함하다
location 현장

love triangles 삼각관계
lyric 가사
make-up 화장
must-have 반드시 가져야 할 것
over and over again 계속 반복해서
phrase 어구
plastic surgery 성형수술
point out 지적하다
popularity 인기
promote 촉진하다
pursue 추구하다
respond 응답하다
revenge 복수
spread 널리 알려지다
survey 설문조사
take measures 조치를 취하다
taste 취향
theme 주제
trend 경향
TV station TV 방송국
warn 경고하다

Grammar Information

I. Verb Tenses(동사 시제)

(1) Regular Verbs(규칙동사)

* 동사가 e로 끝나는 경우는 e를 삭제하고 -ed를 넣는다.

Present (현재)	Past (과거)	Past Participle (과거분사)
fax	faxed	faxed
lock	locked	locked
visit	visited	visited
yell	yelled	yelled
offer	offered	offered
clean	cleaned	cleaned
jump	jumped	jumped
arrive	arrived	arrived
agree	agreed	agreed
decide	decided	decided
search	searched	searched
appear	appeared	appeared
impress	impressed	impressed
destroy	destroyed	destroyed
employ	employed	employed
borrow	borrowed	borrowed
compare	compared	compared
promise	promised	promised

자음이 추가 되는 경우 (단모음과 단자음으로 끝날 때는 자음을 두 번 쓴다.)

rub	rubbed	rubbed
hug	hugged	hugged
stop	stopped	stopped
drop	dropped	dropped

동사가 t/f/r/k +y 로 끝나는 경우는 y를 i로 바꾸고 ed를 넣는다

cry	cried	cried
ski	skied	skied
carry	carried	carried
empty	emptied	emptied
identify	identified	identified

(2) Irregular Verbs(불규칙 동사)

현재, 과거, 과거분사 형이 다른 경우

Present (현재)	Past (과거)	Past Participle (과거분사)
do	did	done
go	went	gone
see	saw	seen
be	was, were	been
begin	began	begun
come	came	come
eat	ate	eaten
fall	fell	fallen
arise	arose	arisen
break	broke	broken
choose	chose	chosen
get	got	gotten
give	gave	given
shake	shook	shaken
speak	spoke	spoken
steal	stole	stolen
take	took	taken
write	wrote	written
draw	drew	drawn
fly	flew	flown
grow	grew	grown
know	knew	known
throw	threw	thrown
ring	rang	rung
sing	sang	sung
swim	swam	swum
wear	wore	worn

과거와 과거분사 형이 같은 경우

bring	brought	brought
buy	bought	bought
catch	caught	caught
fight	fought	fought
teach	taught	taught
think	thought	thought

build	built	built
send	sent	sent
spend	spent	spent
feel	felt	felt
keep	kept	kept
sleep	slept	slept
run	ran	run
sit	sat	sat
sell	sold	sold
tell	told	told
find	found	found
have	had	had
hear	heard	heard
hold	held	held
lead	led	led
leave	left	left
make	made	made
meet	met	met
pay	paid	paid
read	read	read
say	said	said
shoot	shot	shot
stand	stood	stood
win	won	won

현재, 과거, 과거분사형이 같은 경우

cut	cut	cut
hit	hit	hit
let	let	let
set	set	set
cast	cast	cast
cost	cost	cost
hurt	hurt	hurt
put	put	put
quit	quit	quit

II. Adjective (형용사의 원급, 비교급 , 최상급)

1음절 어휘의 형용사의 경우는 −er, −est 를 붙힌다

safe	safer	safest
close	closer	closest
cheap	cheaper	cheapest

cold hard large light nice poor
quick rough fast small wide young

2음절이나 그 이상의 음절의 형용사는 more, most / 또는 less, least (덜 ..하다는 경우)를 형용사 앞에 넣는다.

tired	less tired	least tired
famous	more famous	most famous
beautiful	more beautiful	most beautiful

자음이 추가 되는 경우 (단모음과 단자음으로 끝날 때는 마지막 자음을 하나 더 쓴다.)

big	bigger	biggest
fat	fatter	fattest
thin	thinner	thinnest

hot wet tall sad

2음절 형용사가 y 로 끝나면 y를 i로 바꾸고 −er, −est를 넣는다.

happy	happier	happiest
heavy	heavier	heaviest
pretty	prettier	prettiest

angry busy dirty easy friendly
funny lucky silly tiny lazy

불규칙형

good	better	best
bad	worse	worst
little	less	least
much/many	more	most
old	older/ elder	oldest / eldest
far	farther/further	farthest /furthest